DATE DUE

NOV 15 1999			

ALLEGHENY CAMPUS LIBRARY
COMMUNITY COLLEGE OF ALLEGHENY COUNTY
808 Ridge Avenue
Pittsburgh, Pennsylvania 15212

DEMCO

Suicide Among Young Adults

SUICIDE AMONG YOUNG ADULTS

A. Morgan Parker, Jr., D.Min.

An Exposition-University Book
EXPOSITION PRESS   NEW YORK

HV
6546
.P37

to my wife
Annette
"the" primary significant other
in my life, whose affection
is unfailing

Acknowledgment is hereby given for permission to reprint tables from "Human Violence. A Comparison of Homicide, Aggravated Assault, Suicide, and Attempted Suicide" by Alex D. Pokorny. Reprinted by special permission of the *Journal of Criminal Law, Criminology and Police Science*, © 1965 by Northwestern University School of Law, vol. LVI, 4; and tabular matter from *The Cry for Help* by Norman L. Farberow and Edwin S. Shneidman. © 1965 by McGraw-Hill Book Company. Used with permission of McGraw-Hill Book Company.

The graph on "Number of Suicides" on page 29 is based on a figure in *Suicide Prevention: The Burden of Responsibility* published by Roche Laboratories and used here by permission.

FIRST EDITION

© 1974 by A. Morgan Parker, Jr.

All rights reserved, including the right of reproduction in whole or in part, in any form or by any means, electronic or mechanical, including photocopying, recording, or by any information storage and retrieval system, without permission in writing from the Publisher. Inquiries should be addressed to Exposition Press, Inc., 50 Jericho Turnpike, Jericho, N.Y. 11753

Library of Congress Catalog Card Number: 73-92852

ISBN 0-682-47886-5

Manufactured in the United States of America

Contents

LIST OF TABLES	vii
LIST OF ILLUSTRATIONS	viii
PREFACE	ix
ACKNOWLEDGMENTS	xi

I. **INTRODUCTION** — 1
  Nature of the Problem 1
  Background Attitudes 5
  Definition of Terms 11
  Research Approach 13

II. **OCCURRENCE FACTORS** — 17
  Past and Present 17
  Descriptive Categories 19
    Age 20
    Sex 24
    Race 25
    Religion 26
  Statistical Information 28
    World Wide 32
    United States 34
    Young Adults 37
    Armed Forces 38

III. **CAUSES, DYNAMICS AND MOTIVATIONS** — 44
  Classical Theories 44
    Psychoanalytic 46
    Nonpsychoanalytic 48
  Subsequent Research 50

IV. **SYMPTOMS AND CHARACTERISTICS** — 66
  Verbal Clues 66
  Physical Signs 67
  Personal Actions 69

V. **METHODS OF SUICIDE** — 71
  Both Sexes 71
  Male 73
  Female 76

v

VI.	**CLINICAL FINDINGS**	78
	Focus, Needs, and Design 78	
	Personal Interviews 79	
	Suicide Potential Ratings 88	
	Goals of Life Inventory 94	
	Psychological Autopsies 104	
	Summary and Evaluation of Findings 107	
VII.	**TREATMENT**	110
	Organizationally 110	
	Medically 113	
	Spiritually 116	
	Interpersonally 119	
VIII.	**PREVENTION**	127
	Theological Concepts 127	
	Ethical Considerations 130	
	Educational Concerns 131	
	Facilities Required 133	
IX.	**CONCLUSION**	136
	Applications of the Findings 136	
	Implications for Further Study 141	
	APPENDIX A *Personal Interview Questions*	144
	APPENDIX B *"Goals of Life" Inventory*	
	BIBLIOGRAPHY	151
	INDEX	161

List of Tables

1. Breakdown of Suicides in Physicians by Specialty (May, 1965 to November, 1967) — 19
2. Suicide Rates by Race: United States, 1960, 1969 — 25
3. Religious Preference and Suicide Rates: 1960, 1967 — 27
4. Distribution of Suicide and Attempted Suicide Through Days of the Week — 30
5. Place of Occurrence of Suicides and Attempted Suicides (in percent) — 31
6. Suicides in Selected Countries — 32
7. Age-Adjusted Suicide Rates, by Color and Sex: United States, 1950-64, 1967-69 — 35
8. Suicide Rates by Age: United States, 1950-64, 1968-72 — 36
9. Suicide Rates for United States by Geographic Division, 1967 — 37
10. Suicide Rates: 15-24 years — 39
11. Percentages of Total Psychiatric Patient Population with Suicidal Tendencies: 1964-65 — 58
12. Comparison of Popular Methods of Suicide, 1966-71 — 72
13. Methods of Suicide and Suicide Attempt Both Sexes: United States — 74
14. Methods of Suicide and Suicide Attempt Male: United States — 74
15. Methods of Committed Suicides: 1941-45 — 75
16. Methods of Attempted Suicides, 1964-67 — 76
17. Methods of Suicide and Suicide Attempt Female: United States — 77
18. Methods Used for Committing Suicide: Guns, Hanging, Strangulation, and Barbiturates: United States — 77
19. Personal Interview Questions — 80
20. Tell Me a Little Bit About Yourself — 82
21. Could You Share with Me Something of Your Background? — 83
22. What Was Occurring in Your Life Just Before You Came to the Hospital? — 84
23. What Bearing Has Being in Military Service Had on Your Situation? — 85
24. Is There a Particular Person Or Group of Persons You've Found to Be Especially Helpful to You in This Time? — 87
25. What Are Your Plans and Feelings About the Future? — 87
26. Suicidal Potential Evaluation — 88
27. Positive Replies to Suicidal Potential Evaluation — 89
28. Positive Replies to Suicidal Potential Evaluation by Question — 89
29. High-Low Risk Scale — 91
30. Responses to High Risk-Low Risk Category Scale — 92

31.	Goals of Life	95
32.	Median Score and Rank for "Self"	96
33.	Median Score and Rank for "Others"	98
34.	Median Score for "Self" and "Others"	99
35.	Life Goals Intensity Rating	102
36.	Proposed Suicide Potential Rating for Armed Forces Personnel	142

List of Illustrations

1.	Suicide Rates by Marital Status and Age: 1959-61 (3 year average)	21
2.	Suicide Rates by Age: 1950-64, 1968-69	23
3.	The Seasonal Patterns of Suicidal Deaths, 1964	29
4.	Results High Risk Category Positive Responses	93

Preface

What's a Doctor of Ministry doing writing about suicide? That's often the first question. It's usually followed by others, when I indicate suicide is ultimately a theological problem. When one thinks of taking his life, he or she is asking, "What's my life worth anyway?" or "Is life really worth the hassle?" and "Who really gives a damn anyhow?"

The latter word choice is most likely if the Doctor of Ministry happens to be a Navy Chaplain, as is true in this case, who spends his time hearing the inner cries of people in the armed forces. Those cries are the basis of this exploration into the world of young adult suicide behavior.

That world is a specialized one, but not an isolated one. To perceive what's happening in the young adult world, or any segment of it, is also to perceive the totality of interconnecting human relationships. Broad pictures of suicide occurrence, dynamics and pertinent factors will therefore be surveyed in coming to understand the suicidal young adult both in and out of the armed forces.

In understanding and coping with problems of young adults, we may become increasingly sensitive to initial stages of those problems in early life; and, hopefully, effective in retaining a later life to both understand and enjoy. It's with that hope for us all that this work is offered. May it not only give us "Courage To Be" in this troublesome world, but insights into how we might be meaningfully and creatively ALIVE.

Acknowledgments

Deepest appreciation is extended to the forty patients of both the suicide and control group who shared generously of their time, personal lives, and meaningful insights in order to make this effort possible. Prayerful wishes for future well-being are especially with the suicide patients who shared of their "cry for help" in hopes that others would be saved from moments of desperation.

To the chaplains, physicians, psychiatrists, corpsmen, and other hospital personnel who rendered vital support and assistance in this research, gratitude is most sincerely extended.

The Surgeon Generals of the Army, Navy, and Air Force deserve special thanks for the research, correspondence and enthusiastic encouragement they gave to the study. The commands of both the National Naval Medical Center in Bethesda, Maryland, and Portsmouth Naval Hospital, Portsmouth, Virginia, were also vitally instrumental and supportive in this research study. The Senior Chaplain of the National Naval Medical Center, Captain John Vincer, assisted in research arrangements and gave constant support to the study, for which heartfelt thanks is expressed.

Long, patient, and invaluable guidance to this work was provided by Dr. Tibor Chikes, the major advisor, and Dr. Ray Fitzgerald, reader and advisor. No medium can express the measure of gratitude extended to these gentlemen.

Others who rendered valuable assistance to this probing search include: Mr. Gerald Myer, Miss Carol Ann Stephens, and Miss Gary Turner of the Stitt Memorial Library of the National Naval Medical Center; Mr. Berkley Hathorne of the NIMH Center for Suicide Studies in Washington, D.C.; and Mrs. Jean Fitzgerald for proofreading and form assistance.

And finally, the constant and untiring labors of my wife,

Annette, in statistical computations and typing, have made it possible for the completed work to be accomplished. Her devotions to this labor have certainly been "above and beyond the call," and more than deserving of any gratitude which can possibly be expressed.

1. Introduction

NATURE OF THE PROBLEM

Army Private David S. Swanson, twenty-one, was found dead in his bed at home in New Britain, Connecticut, on Sunday, September 21, 1969. According to the story reported in *The Washington Post,* Swanson had died of an overdose of sleeping pills.[1] Prior to his death the young Army Private had slashed his wrists twice and had been interviewed by psychiatrists, his first sergeant, company commander, and chaplain. They thought he "could adjust."

On Saturday, January 24, 1970, Caroline Schutz, a seventeen year old French girl, set herself afire and jumped blazing from her fourth-floor schoolroom to the Paris street below. The press report indicated she was the fifth person to die by self-immolation in France within a week.[2] Three of the five were young adults, seventeen and eighteen years of age.

Other news releases remind us almost daily of the shocking and increasing tragedy of self-destructive acts both at home and around the world. It is particularly disturbing to note an apparent upsurge of such acts among the young adult population. Studies will be later examined which indicate that this age group is presently registering the highest percentage increase of committed suicides.

Yet the problem of suicide and attempted suicide touches all people of all ages. Dr. Karl Menninger says, "Once every minute or even more often, someone in the United States either kills himself or tries to kill himself with conscious intent."[3] At least sixty Americans will have taken their own lives by this time tomorrow. More than 22,000 persons in the United States killed themselves last year, and nine times that many attempted suicide.[4] For every known attempted suicide there are three to four persons who reportedly make an attempt on their life that is not recorded. And many of those who attempted will try again, a number with lethal success.

In this country alone one begins to see a problem which may well annually touch as many as 200,000 to 300,000 of every age and walk of life. Few people realize that suicide is more frequent than murder and more easily predicted, according to Shneidman and Farberow's *Clues To Suicide*.[5] This factor of predictability is a crucial concern of all engaged in the newly designated field of "Suicidology."[6] It shall receive particular attention in our study of young adults in the Armed Forces.

Predictability becomes increasingly important when another factor of research is made known. Except for a very few, all of the people who commit suicide want desperately to live.[7] Shneidman and Farberow's classic, *The Cry for Help*, is an indication of this basic factor to remember in confronting the suicidal. Amid the complexities of a most complicated phenomenon, the suicidal person is reaching out for help and is as anxious to find meaningful life as he is to let go of life.

Despite this desire to live, suicide continues to occur at such rates as to distinctly mark it as a major national and international mental health problem. In the United States, suicide ranks as the eleventh highest cause of death for all age groups. Among young adults it ranks as the fifth highest. It is the third most common cause of death between fifteen and nineteen years of age. Suicide now outranks pneumonia, polio, tuberculosis, diabetes, rheumatic fever, kidney disease, appendicitis, and leukemia as a cause of death in teenagers. On college campuses today, suicide is second only to accidents as a cause of death.[8] The Memorial Hospital of Long Beach indicates that approximately 40 per cent of the calls coming in on the Counseling Services Help Now Telephone Line are from persons contemplating suicide.[9]

With this extensive and dramatically serious situation, one is a little surprised to discover that, in the words of one doctor, "scientific research on the subject of suicide is remarkably rare and that few subjects are as widely distorted by misconception and misunderstanding."[10] Indeed, after a search of the literature, it would seem that following original classics, little advancement in understanding and prevention of suicide took place until the

Introduction

1950's. More has been done to mobilize study and resources in positive programs of suicide prevention within the past two decades than had been undertaken for centuries before. This jolting assertion becomes increasingly verified as one begins to realize how most centuries of the past were repeated lessons in regression with regard to treatment of the suicidal and their families.

Dr. Schneidman sharpens the picture with regard to lack of information when he says there are only five facts about suicide that we presently know for certain. They are: (a) its remediation is unknown; we don't know exactly how to cure it; (b) its etiology is unknown; we don't know what causes it; (c) its nature is unknown; we don't what it is, if it is an it, which it obviously isn't; (d) individuals continue to present themselves labelled with this diagnosis; and (e) individuals in our society responsible for treatment have no choice but to continue to diagnose and treat it the best they can—within the limitations indicated above.[11]

One looking at suicide and attempted suicide even within this century and within recent years still finds himself doing a good bit of head scratching. Is it any wonder then that suicide has horrified and fascinated men from antiquity to the present time? After all, all animals can kill, but only man decides to kill himself. Perhaps it is this factor which prompts Albert Camus in *Le Mythe de Sisyphe* to say, "there is only one really serious philosophical problem, and this is suicide."[12] It is a problem that has been with man from the beginning. Stengel observes that it has been found to occur in every society in all history.[13] Only small, isolated groups of primitive peoples have been thought, by some researchers, to be free of suicide. Even there, lack of information may be as equally supportive of occurrence as against it. While sometimes referred to as "the curse of the poor" or the "disease of the rich," it is in reality a most "democratic" problem which is represented fairly proportionately through all levels of society.[14]

Furthermore, Meerloo implies that every disgruntled being plays with thoughts of hara-kiri at one time or another, as his mind says to him, "Either my will and wishes are gratified or I choose death."[15] In a curious twist, there are those who've even cited suicide as the last freedom. History amply records how such thoughts, mixed with fear and guilt, have led not only individuals but entire groups of people into mass self-destruction. A pointed example was evidenced in certain eighteenth century Russian religious sects whose special aim was suicide. Their self-killing in shifts, apparently stimulated by hidden fears, is still known as Russian Roulette.[16]

Another aspect of this problem, which will come under fuller examination later, is introduced by Freud's early statement that "Death is the aim of all life."[17] This has led to some interesting conclusions as men have built upon this conviction. James Hillman says for instance, "Going to the end in analysis means going to death and starting from there. If death is life's goal, then death is more basic than life itself. If a choice must be made between the two, then life must yield to its goal."[18] Dr. Hillman, in a strange fashion, thus exalts death over life. Only the dying, he says, are really alive; life takes its value through death.

Obviously, there are a variety of views concerning just what suicide is, what it means to individuals and society, and what constructive efforts can or should be taken to assist the suicidal patient. When focus is specifically directed toward the young adult serving in the armed forces, additional considerations become important. Not only is an individual's life at stake, but the lives of untold numbers around him may depend upon the stability of one man. One military doctor relates this in quite matter-of-fact fashion in saying, "Suicidal reactions in Service conditions are seen to be wasteful of potential manpower, and detrimental to unit morale."[19] Indeed, the entire mission involving thousands of lives could be jeopardized by a key man turning to self-destruction. The difference between major victory or defeat, especially in modern technological warfare, might be decided by an act of suicide.

Yet it is surprising to see what little study has been devoted to the problem of suicide in the armed forces. A few scattered journal articles, generally quite brief, comprise the main body of material. Since the armed forces are, in the main, composed of young adults, whose suicide rates are rising, the need for increased study is obvious. Hopefully, insightful discoveries in this one group could have important implications for both military and civilians of all ages.

Introduction

Is there a special concern and contribution by the chaplain in this struggle for men's lives? And beyond him, is the Christian Church as a whole in a position to offer a ministry to young people at life's ultimate moment of choice? These questions will underlie the entire inquiry ahead and prompt some specific responses where appropriate.

Vast, untamed, and complicated as suicidal behavior may be, it is imperative to openly come to terms with it, bringing the full resources of all helpful disciplines, for as Dr. Mathew Ross assures us, "suicidal risk is recognizable, predictable and preventable."[20] It is under the stimulus of these assurances that this study proceeds with the hope of gleaning additional directions for constructive and redemptive ministries to the person coping with suicidal tendencies.

BACKGROUND ATTITUDES

Dr. E. G. Morhauser reminds us that suicide and attempted suicide have long been complex phenomena about which folkways, mores, taboos, and laws of culture and subculture have revolved.[21] While reactions have varied greatly from one culture to another, the predominant attitude, especially for Western man, has been one of dismay, horror, and revulsion when dealing with suicide.

This attitude is based, in large part, says St. John-Stevas, on a legacy of centuries of Christian teaching which see in suicide the worst of all sins, that of despair.[22] To the Christian, suicide has been viewed as rejection of both God and man. It has been interpreted as a denial of God's sovereign providence and as a throwing back at Him of the gift of life. At the same time, it has been perceived as an act of no-confidence in one's fellow man.

This attitude is reported to have differed greatly from the pagan indifference of the Greek and Roman world. While suicide may not have been generally accepted or very widely practiced, still there were special groups such as the Stoics who felt suicide could liberate them from the anxiety of fate and death.[23]

To perceive the beginnings of attitudes toward suicide, though, one must go back before the Christian or Greek and Roman period. Fedden reminds us that it is rather to the works of magic and primitive religion found in African tribes and Australian aborigines that one must look.[24] There one learns of the primitive taboo which is the origin of the suicide horror. Taboo itself rested in a "power" which permeated everything. The power could be good or evil. Unnatural death produced fears of ghosts, concepts of uncleanness, and desire to shed oneself of any blood guilt. Thus was imparted to succeeding centuries feelings of one possessed by an unclean power, a demon spirit, or becoming taboo and a need to control and separate oneself from this crazed or "power" driven evil.

In contrast, it's interesting to note that suicide cases reported in the Old Testament were not under condemnation of the writers. The reports included: (1) Samson (Judges 16:27-30), (2) Saul (I Sam. 31:4), (3) Saul's Armorbearer (I Sam. 31:5), (4) Zimri (I Kings 16:15-18), (5) Ahithophel (II Sam. 16:23-17:23). Jewish opposition to suicide appeared to come later, with the emphasis on life and God's providence.[25]

The one New Testament suicide story left strong negative impact, however. Remembrance of Judas brought thoughts of terror and cowardliness. This, no doubt, contributed to the early church's conviction about suicide as expressed by St. Augustine in *City of God*. He offered these three reasons for opposition to suicide: (1) It precluded any opportunity for repentance, (2) Scripture commanded "Thou shalt not kill," and (3) It is a cowardly act. Life is to be faced more like Job than Judas.[26] Augustine apparently posited as an only exception, the saints who committed such acts under divine inspiration.

While Augustine denounced suicide as a sin, Thomas Acquinas gave the impression that it was a crime. He described suicide in the threefold fashion: (1) A sin against nature, (2) Against the community, and (3) Against God.[27] He established his position upon what he felt were fundamental Christian doctrines dealing with the sacredness of life and submission to God's will, which were fundamental to the Jewish and Mohammendan position as well.

It was in A.D. 452, at the Council of Arles, that the Christian Church adopted prohibition of suicide saying, "whoever kills himself, thereby killing an innocent person, commits homicide."[28] Thus the criminal and the victim were combined in one person. In explaining this position, it was often indicated that we must love ourselves as we do our neighbors. The Council of Toledo in

Introduction

A.D. 693 decided upon excommunication of the suicide and denial of Christian burial.[29] This decision initiated reactions continuing to this day regarding burial in consecrated ground, types of funeral rites available, and general public as well as legal attitudes toward suicide.

From the Middle Ages until comparatively recently, indignities were practiced on the corpse of the suicide. Not only was the body not placed in the churchyard cemetery, but it was often dragged through the streets, hung on public gallows and left for carrion birds to destroy—after a stake had been driven through the heart.[30] Superstitions were rampant about the suicide's corpse and ghost. According to Whalley:

> They could create famine, make the earth barren, produce hail, tempest or drought, haunt people viciously. If a pregnant woman stepped on the grave of a suicide her child would eventually follow the same bitter path. Often suicides were buried at the crossroads, where constant traffic would keep the ghost down.[31]

Perhaps because of such attitudes, suicide decreased greatly during the Middle Ages. Self-destruction was obviously made most unpopular, thereby bringing about in strange fashion a rather effective suicide prevention program. Since theological and civil authority were inseparable, effective deterrents were thus widely employed.

New thought currents began to develop about the fourteenth century, however, which were in considerable evidence by the seventeenth century. Men such as John Donne argued that "self-homicide was a sin against the law of self-preservation, but no more."[32] Hume, Montesquieu, Voltaire, Rousseau, wrote essays defending suicide under certain conditions. All argued for freedom of the individual over ecclesiastical authorities.

English common law of the eighteenth century considered suicide a crime punishable by denial of a Christian burial, sanctions imposed upon the corpse (buried in the highway with a stake driven through the body), and confiscation of property.[33] Obviously new thought currents emphasizing individual freedom were much in the minority. Indeed, Canon law regarding suicide appeared to strongly influence all continental European laws.

French law of 1270 declared the property of the suicide and his wife escheated to the Lord. A custom of Brittany called for the suicide to be hanged by his feet, dragged through the streets "as a murderer," and that his chattels be forfeited.[34] Similar laws and customs could be found in force through Italy, Germany, and Austria until the eighteenth century and even in the early nineteenth century. Sanctions imposed upon suicide were not abrogated in Austria until 1850.[35] Attempted suicide was punishable by law in England in 1854, and not until August 1961, was suicide removed as a felony under English law.[36]

In the United States, the English common law on suicide was never accepted with its full implications. Yet in New York State, suicide was a crime until 1919. New York and Oregon have since indicated by legislative action that suicide is "a grave public wrong."[37] The four states of New York, California, Missouri, and Wisconsin recognize as specific criminal offense the act of assisting someone in suicide.[38]

This long history of social, theological, and legal opposition to suicide has been matched, as indicated briefly, by small group and individual efforts pointing in another direction. Many modern existentialists have indicated that life in which man could not kill himself would be something other than life. Voicing the "last freedom" theme they say the possibility of suicide is the mark of humanity.[39]

The Reverend Robert Capon, in his delightful book, *Bed and Board,* offers this distinctly "open" attitude toward suicide:

> Life is not intelligible. The carefully planned steps that people take to fix it up are intelligible enough: Divorce is intelligible and contraception is intelligible and adjustment is intelligible and suicide is intelligible. But reality is not. The whole of being is precisely absurd. Only the wholesale acceptance of the nonsense of actuality is sane.[40]

If one turns to an examination of other cultures outside the Western world, there is an immediate impression of strange attitudes toward suicide. The early cultures of our own American Indians present a striking example of mingled attitudes. The Kwakiutl Indians of the northwest coast were ashamed at the occurrence of all accidents.[41] If a man lost at gambling and was

Introduction

stripped of his property, he had the recourse of suicide. Apparently the choice was a frequent one. If the Plains Indians saw nothing ahead that looked attractive, they could take a year's suicide pledge. A peculiar buckskin badge eight feet long was worn in battle which was attached by a stake to one particular position from which one could not retreat. If by chance one survived the year, he won all kinds of recognition. Among the Pueblos, suicide was entirely outlawed as much too violent an act to contemplate. Homicide occurred so seldom it could hardly be remembered.[42] Here at one time, in fairly similar cultures, it is possible to observe attitudes of casual acceptance or total rejection of suicide. Cultural acceptance, however, appears as the dominant characteristic.

A shift to the nation of India presents an even more dramatic acceptance of suicide. As once commonly practiced in India by all classes of people, suicide was not regarded as a sin, but rather a meritorious act. Wives voluntarily died on the funeral pyres of their husbands, while records of the deed were often preserved in stone or metal.[43] These personal acts of "Suttee" were pursued en masse as "Jouhar" when thousands of defeated warriors' wives would immolate themselves to preserve their honor in face of defeat by the enemy. Māmakham was the great sacrifice in which subjects swore to their king that upon his death they would take their own lives.[44] This was done before the entire population of the city. There were also constant processions to sacred waterways where the Indian who drowned himself while remaining pure looked to the hope of being reborn as a king.

This honoring and elevating of suicide has been noted more recently among the Japanese "harakiri" in which suicide is not a crime but rather a means of eradicating a crime. By his suicide, the accused remained "innocent" and thus regained social respect.[45] While suicide motives have reportedly changed in modern Japan, it is still interesting to note their very high rates. The impact of history apparently weighs heavily upon those whose ancestors were the Samurai warriors who disemboweled themselves to win esteem or the Kamakazi pilots who gained glory in giving all.

An interesting attitude of employing suicide can be found among the contemporary Buddhists of Vietnam. Suicide is reported as a not uncommon practice in which someone is told the reasons for such drastic action, either verbally or by a note setting forth grievances. Ancient Vietnamese law incriminates those who are considered the cause of such suicide and classifies it as "murder by oppression."[46]

Among other primitive peoples, South Sea islanders such as the Trobriands and fairly unexplored cultures like the Eskimos, one finds suicide at work restoring esteem, reducing shame, or simply terminating old age. The rejected tribesman setting forth by canoe to ultimate destiny, the native plunging himself from palm tree top, or the arctic dweller simply walking away into the frozen wasteland, all tell of amazing attitudes with which men have handled life by destroying self.

The military environment has embraced particular attitudes through history toward self-destruction. The Roman emperors regarded attempted suicide in their legionaries as equivalent to desertion and therefore a punishable offence.[47] Roman Law stated the death penalty could be imposed for attempted suicide when no obviously strong reason was known for the act.

Napoleon issued the following General Order from St. Cloud: "To abandon oneself to grief without resisting, and to kill oneself in order to escape from it, is like abandoning the field of battle before conquering it."[48]

In Britain, the Army Act of 1881 (section 38) attempted to discourage would-be suicides by cashiering officer offenders and sentencing other ranks to two years imprisonment with hard labor.[49]

The Asiatic soldier, as indicated in the description of Japanese attitudes, accepted suicide with equanimity which frequently gave rise to epidemics of imitative and ritual self-immolation. His was a different pattern among military traditions.

In our own American Armed Forces the threat of suicide has usually been regarded as an urgent psychiatric emergency, and as a situation most calculated to disrupt normal military routine. The would-be suicide is most often in an isolation created by emotional barriers between himself and the rest of his unit along with medical separation. A completed act most often provokes a fleeting sensation, some mild speculation, a formal inquiry and perhaps a few uninformative lines in the press.[50] The attempt which fails represents a standing threat to the spiritual ease and integrity of the organization, for it becomes aware of special faults and stresses which threaten life.

In tracing previous attitudes toward suicide through history and in different cultures, one comes to see the variety of reactions men have exhibited to this deed of finality. While, in a sense, the inheritors of the past, our own culture has steered a course not altogether like its predecessor's. The course of America's attitude toward suicide has not been very specifically delineated. The silence has tended to foster taboo reactions, which only of late are being examined and possibly revised. This continuing enterprise of examination will occupy us in a later chapter.

DEFINITION OF TERMS

It's surprising to note that the word "suicide" is itself of fairly recent origin.[51] Though apparently from Latin, it corresponds to no Latin word, for the Romans used paraphrases to express the thought. Phrases such as *sibi mortem consciscere*—to procure his own death; *vim sibi inferre*—to cause violence to himself; or *sua manu cadere*—to fall by his own hand, are the commonest expressions. In England the early name for suicide seems to have been self-homicide, which reflected something of the legal attitude. The word "suicide" first appears about the middle of the seventeenth century. In Edward Philipp's *New World of Words*, published in 1662, one finds the following:

> One barbarous word I shall produce, which is "suicide," a word which I had rather should be derived from *sus*, a sow, than from the pronoun *sui*, unless there be some mystery in it; as if it were a swinish part for a man to kill himself.[52]

To impart appropriate meaning to this term of recent origin and to the host of expressions related to it shall now be our task.

Suicide is described in the classical and probably best known work on the subject, Durkheim's *Le Suicide*, as the "term applied to all cases of death resulting directly or indirectly from a positive or negative act of the victim himself, which he knows will produce this result."[53] It is defined by physicians as "a deliberate act of self-injury aimed at self-destruction,"[54] and as "a violent self-inflicted destructive action resulting in death."[55]

For expanded meanings, it would be well to remember Shneidman and Farberow's words, "Suicide itself is more a way of 'living'—in which the distinguishing feature is that the termination of living is self-administered."[56] Dr. Berblinger says, "Transposed into communication, suicide constitutes a message. It may represent a message to which no answer is expected, it may implicitly call for a reply, and it may indicate that no solution seems possible."[57]

Various types of suicide will now be defined, followed by definitions for self-destructive behavior which does not result in death.

Chronic Suicide as defined by Menninger is that slow suicide which one commits "by inches."[58] It is the self-destruction practiced by the ascetic, hypochondriacs, neurotic invalids, and alcohol addicts.

Focal Suicide is concentrated upon the body and usually upon a limited part of the body. Forms of self-mutilation, purposive accidents (auto and pedestrian), sexual impotence and compulsive surgery are typical of this type.[59]

Organic Suicide is replacing an external cross with an internal one.[60] This exhibits itself in boils, diseases, guilt producing genitalurinary complications, and even eye problems.

Intentional Suicide is thought to be a consciously directed self-inflicted injury.[61]

Semi-intentional Suicide is that unconscious intention to carry out self-destruction which may be masked as a casual mishap.[62]

Concealed Suicide is that suicide which is camouflaged as natural death after sickness or camouflaged as murder.[63]

Undiscovered Suicide refers to those who carried out suicide but are considered "disappeared" or "missing."[64]

Social Suicide is committed by some people with their behavior in society as in sexual escapades, or even business failure.[65]

Attempted Suicide has been treated in the past by many as though it were simply different dimensions of factors involved in suicide. Recently, however, the view has emerged that attempted suicide may represent very different phenomena from suicide—not only descriptively, but etiologically and dynamically as well.[66] Basically, attempted suicide is described as a "determined and serious intention of killing oneself" which is without fatal termina-

Introduction

tion, usually because unsuitable or inadequate means are being used unknowingly.[67]

While a self-destructive intention is carried out, the attempter is most often actually more interested in improving life than terminating it. The act may be seen more as a "moving toward others" than withdrawing as in suicide.[68] Thus it becomes a cry for help.

Suicidal Gesture is an act considered similar to attempted suicide, except that persons performing such an action "neither intend to end life nor expect to die as a result of their action."[69] Such gestures are often impulsive or premeditated acts with a theatrical attention-seeking element. Some physicians would feel that "the distinction between suicide gesture and suicide attempt should not necessarily be based on the seriousness of the medical consequences of the action but more on the psychodynamics of the action."[70]

Suicidal Threat is a statement of intention to suicide, but no relevant action is performed.[71] It is often thought to be a form of moral blackmail, usually to intimidate authority figures, with frustration, resentment, and conscious guilt as precipitating factors.[72]

Suicidal Ideation takes place when the person thinks, talks, or writes about suicide without expressing any definite intent of performing any relevant action.[73] This might well include those who, because of anxiety and fears, express ruminations, preoccupations, and obsessions of self-destruction.

Suicidal Behavior or *Intent* may be used to refer to one or more of the preceding categories in the broad range of self-destructive activity.[74] Since virtually any of these could lead to completed suicide, it is imperative for those working with the suicidal[75] to perceive progression from one level to another and to realize that by accident low risk incidents could prove fatal.

RESEARCH APPROACH

This study of young adults between the ages of seventeen and twenty-five who have attempted or committed suicide in the United States Armed Forces is designed as an exploratory descriptive analysis. The purpose of this investigation will be to examine a little explored subject, in an almost unexplored context, with the hope of discerning significant factors in understanding and dealing with suicidal behavior. A special focus will be directed to the role of the chaplain and the Christian ministry, in general, as vital resources in suicide prevention.

After setting forth the problem with attention to attitudes of the past, the study will proceed to examine theories regarding the nature of suicide, occurrence data, its symptoms and methods employed in attempting suicide.

Clinical research then follows, based upon personal interviews with twenty military suicidal patients and the same number of general medical military patients, matched and randomly selected. Beyond subjective descriptions of key factors in suicidal dynamics, objective inventories will explore life's attitudes, personality characteristics, and long range goals. The religious dimension will receive special attention. Suicide prediction scales will be employed and evaluated. Finally, psychological autopsies will be conducted for discovery of causation and possible future prevention.

A summary of findings will be the basis for proposals in treatment and prevention of suicide in the armed forces. Hopefully the applications and implications for future work and research will be meaningful not only in the military or among young adults, but may, in fact, have value for all age groups in every sector of society.

NOTES

1. Bernard D. Nossiter, "Suicide Ends GI's Cry: 'I Can't Stand All This . . . ,'" *The Washington Post* (Washington, D.C.), September 25, 1969, p. A4.

2. UPI, "Paris Girl, 17, Sets Self Ablaze, Leaps to Death," *The Sunday Star* (Washington, D.C.), January 25, 1970, Sec. C, p. 12.

3. "Suicide," Information Bulletin of Memorial Hospital of Long Beach, California, Pastoral Counseling Center (n.d.), p. 2.

4. Edwin S. Shneidman and Philip Mandelkorn, *How to Prevent Suicide,* in Public Affairs Pamphlet No. 406 (Washington, 1968), p. 1.

5. Edwin S. Shneidman and Norman T. Farberow, eds., *Clues to Suicide* (New York: McGraw-Hill Book Company, Inc., 1957), p. v.

6. A new specialty for study and treatment of suicidal individuals which Stanley F. Yolles, Director of NIMH, calls "a uniquely interdisciplinary profession, involving individuals with a wide variety of backgrounds in science, medicine, health, and allied fields."

Introduction

7. Schneidman and Mandelkorn, *How to Prevent Suicide*, p. 1.

8. Harris C. Faigel, "Suicide Among Young Persons," *Clinical Pediatrics*, V (March, 1966), p. 187.

9. "Memorial Counseling Center," Information Sheet of Memorial Hospital of Long Beach, California, Department of Pastoral Care (n.d.), p. 8. (Mimeographed.)

10. Henry B. Bruyn and Richard H. Seiden, "Student Suicide: Fact or Fancy," *Journal of the American College Health Association*, XIV (December, 1965), p. 69.

11. Elsa A. Whalley, "Religion and Suicide," Bureau of Research and Survey National Council of Churches (February, 1964), p. 4. (Mimeographed.)

12. Norman St. John-Stevas, *The Right to Life* (New York: Holt, Rinehart and Winston, 1964), p. 55.

13. Erwin Stengel, *Suicide and Attempted Suicide* (Baltimore, Maryland: Penguin Books, 1964), p. 12.

14. Merville O. Vincent, "Suicide and How to Prevent It," *Christianity Today*, X (1969), p. 346.

15. Joost A. M. Meerloo, *Suicide and Mass Suicide* (New York: Grune and Stratton, Inc., 1962), p. 4.

16. *Ibid.*, p. 72.

17. *Ibid.*, p. 20.

18. "Doctor Death," *The Times Literary Supplement* (New York, March 4, 1965), p. 167.

19. Captain A. R. K. Mitchell, "Suicidal Reaction in the Service Environment," *Journal of the Royal Army Medical Corps*, CIX (1963), p. 219.

20. Mathew Ross, "Suicide Among College Students," *American Journal of Psychiatry*, CXXVI (August, 1969), p. 106.

21. E. G. Morhauser, "Suicide" (Unpublished study for Medical Corps, United States Navy, n.d.), p. 1.

22. St. John-Stevas, *The Right to Life*, p. 55.

23. Paul Tillich, *The Courage to Be* (New Haven: Yale University Press, 1952), p. 55.

24. Henry R. Fedden, *Suicide* (London: Peter Davies Limited, 1938), p. 32.

25. St. John-Stevas, *The Right to Life*, p. 58.

26. *Ibid.*, p. 59.

27. Whalley, "Religion and Suicide," p. 25.

28. Shneidman and Farberow, eds., *Clues to Suicide*, p. 80.

29. *Ibid.*, p. 81.

30. Whalley, "Religion and Suicide," p. 25.

31. *Ibid.*

32. *Ibid.*, p. 26.

33. Shneidman and Farberow, eds., *Clues to Suicide*, p. 81.

34. *Ibid.*, p. 82.
35. *Ibid.*, p. 84.
36. Meerloo, *Suicide and Mass Suicide*, p. 8.
37. St. John-Stevas, *The Right to Life*, p. 70.
38. Shneidman and Farberow, *Clues to Suicide*, p. 89.
39. Seward Hiltner, "The Pastor and Suicide Prevention: An Editorial," *Pastoral Psychology*, XVII, No. 160 (1966), p. 28.
40. Robert Farrar Capon, *Bed and Board* (New York: Simon and Schuster, Inc., 1965), p. 154.
41. Ruth Benedict, *Patterns of Culture* (New York: Houghton Mifflin Company, 1934), p. 215.
42. *Ibid.*, p. 117.
43. Benjamin Walker, *The Hindu World* (New York: Frederick A. Praeger, 1968), p. 446.
44. *Ibid.*, p. 447.
45. Edwin S. Shneidman, *Essays in Self-Destruction* (New York: Science House, Inc., 1967), p. 230.
46. Robert L. Mole, "Vietnamese Buddhism" (unpublished Navy Personal Response Project Officer Report, COMNAVSUPPACT, Saigon, FPO, San Francisco, California, 96214), p. A-1. (n.d.)
47. Harry Pozner, "Suicidal Incidents In Military Personnel," *The British Journal of Psychology*, XLIV (May, 1953), p. 94.
48. Henry Romilly Fedden, *Suicide* (London: Peter Davies Limited, 1938), p. 243.
49. Pozner, "Suicidal Incidents In Military Personnel," p. 94.
50. *Ibid.*
51. Fedden, *Suicide*, p. 29.
52. *Ibid.*
53. Emile Durkheim, *Suicide* (Glencoe, Illinois: The Free Press, 1951), p. 42.
54. Faigel, "Suicide Among Young Persons," p. 187.
55. Morhauser, "Suicide," p. 2.
56. Edwin S. Shneidman and Norman L. Farberow, "Suicide and Death," in *The Meaning of Death*, ed. by Herman Feifel (New York: McGraw-Hill Book Company, Inc., 1959), p. 284.
57. Klaus W. Berblinger, "Suicide as a Message," *Psychosomatics*, V (1964), p. 145.
58. Karl A. Menninger, *Man Against Himself* (New York: Harcourt, Brace and Company, 1938), p. 87.
59. *Ibid.*, p. 229.
60. *Ibid.*, p. 363.
61. Beulah Chamberlain Bosselman, *Self-Destruction* (Springfield, Illinois: Charles C. Thomas Publisher, 1958), p. vii.
62. *Ibid.*
63. Klaus Thomas, "Marriage Counseling, Suicide Prevention and

Pastoral Care," Lectures given at Wesley Theological Seminary, Washington D.C. (August 15, 1965), p. 58. (Mimeographed.)

64. *Ibid.*

65. Roche Laboratories, *Suicide Prevention: The Burden of Responsibility* (Nutley, New Jersey: Roche Laboratories, n.d.), p. 5.

66. Lynnette Beall, "The Dynamics of Suicide: A Review of the Literature, 1897-1965," *Bulletin of Suicidology* (March, 1969), p. 4.

67. Thomas, "Marriage Counseling, Suicide Prevention, and Pastoral Care," p. 58.

68. Alex D. Pokorny, "Human Violence: A Comparison of Homicide, Aggravated Assault, Suicide, and Attempted Suicide," *The Journal of Criminal Law, Criminology and Police Science*, LVI, No. 4 (1965), p. 489.

69. Morhauser, "Suicide," p. 2.

70. Gary J. Tucker and E. R. Gorman, "The Significance of the Suicide Gesture in the Military," *American Journal of Psychiatry*, CXXIII, No. 7 (1967), p. 854.

71. Morhauser, "Suicide," p. 2.

72. Pozner, "Suicidal Incidents In Military Personnel," p. 97.

73. Morhauser, "Suicide," p. 2.

74. Leston L. Havens, "Diagnosis of Suicidal Intent," *Annual Review of Medicine*, XX (1969), p. 419.

75. Throughout this search the words suicidal and suicide will be found in noun form to designate the person or persons reflecting suicidal tendencies or carrying out suicidal activity. This usage is consistent with authoritative writings by Shneidman, Mandelkorn, Farberow, Beall, and Knight with regard to suicidal, and with Shneidman, Faigel, Whalley, Farberow, and Yolles in reference to suicide.

2. Occurrence Factors

PAST AND PRESENT

The true incidence of suicide has always been difficult to ascertain. Varying methods of certifying causes of death, different registration and coding procedures, and a variety of other factors have complicated objective classification.[1] Perhaps the most significant factor in recording suicide incidence has been the cultural attitude toward suicide.

Without a doubt, the actual number of committed suicides has always been far greater than the incidence recorded. We can reasonably assume that any error in reporting will result from too conservative a representation. This results in part from the stigma against suicide imposed because of religious conviction, social disgrace, or personal guilt. Prejudice against admission of suicide brings kindly men, Dr. Yolles suggests, to such falsehoods, as, "He died accidentally while cleaning his gun."[2]

Yet, even ignoring the "concealed suicides," the scope of our concerns is of huge proportion. Suicide has horrified and fascinated men from antiquity to the present time. But while men have elected to die in all periods of history, never have so many done so as in the present. Suicide has spread throughout the twentieth century.[3] The world figure is estimated to possibly exceed half a million a year.

Recent decades have been considered to be a time when suicide was on the increase. In 1959, it was eleventh most common cause of death on the North American continent; while in Scotland the suicide rate increased 50 per cent between 1950 and 1960.[4]

On the other hand, suicide occurrence is apparently not as widespread in some areas today as it was in previous periods. In the United States, for instance, much higher rates than the present 11.7 per 100,000 annually were experienced during the depression years when as high as 17.4 per 100,000 was recorded.[5] It's also noteworthy that in practically every country suicide declines during wartime. In the United States the suicide rate dropped by one-third from 1915 to 1920, the period of World War I, and dropped again by one-third in the World War II years 1943 and 1944.[6]

It perhaps comes as a slight jolt in the western world to discover neither medicine nor other scientific advancement have curbed suicide. Nor has economic growth through technology retarded occurrence of this problem; if anything, it has possibly increased it.[7]

Some assurance can be found in the rather consistent nature of this problem. Except for the periods mentioned, economic depression and war, the suicide rates in any particular country generally follow the pattern of previous rates in that country.[8]

Suicide has tended to be more frequent in urban rather than rural areas, with the very highest rates occurring in the largest cities.[9] However, the gap between these two areas has been closing of late.

While suicide rates have increased during economic crisis, it is important to understand that suicide is not particularly associated with the poor.[10] Though a completely destitute person might be driven in despair to consider self-destruction, statistics apparently indicate all economic levels are fairly equally exposed to actual occurrence.

Some persons within each economic level are particularly prone to suicide, though; and to those we now give attention.

DESCRIPTIVE CATEGORIES

Among professions, the highest suicide rates are found in the medical field. Physicians and dentists as a whole average a rate of at least 33 per 100,000—double the rate for white American males. For psychiatrists, the rate has been found to be at least 61 per 100,000—four times the white male population (see Table 1).[11] Other professionals such as teachers and clergymen have uniformly very low suicide rates. While further analysis may pro-

TABLE 1

Breakdown of Suicides in Physicians by Specialty (May, 1965 to November, 1967)*

Specialty	Rate per 100,000 population
Psychiatrists	61
Ophthalmologists	55
Anesthesiologists	52
Obstetrician-Gynecologists	36
General Practitioners	34
Radiologists	27
Pediatricians	10

*P. H. Blachly, William Disher, and Gregory Roduner, "Suicide By Physicians," *Bulletin of Suicidology* (December, 1968), p. 5.

duce clearer readings in the future, researchers tend to indicate skilled workers below the U.S. national average of 11 per 100,000 and unskilled and agricultural laborers above the national rate.[12]

College students have presented alarming suicide rates with many U.S. colleges similar to the University of California's ratings of 17.4 per 100,000; Oxford University has posted rates as high as 59.4 per 100,000.[13]

Suicide rates are higher among the mentally ill than in the normal population, with data suggesting about 15 per cent of persons suffering from depressive illnesses may eventually die by suicide.[14]

Foremost among those likely to commit suicide are those who have already made one or more attempts. Some studies show that an average of 5 per cent of these who've attempted, will kill themselves within five years of their first attempt while up to 10 per cent will do so over long periods.[15]

Marital status is the final of these special limited categories which has an important relationship to suicide rates. For single persons the rate per 100,000 as recorded most recently by the National Center for Health Statistics is 20.9 (33.2 for males and 7.7 for females); for married persons, 11.9; for the widowed, the rate is 23.8, and for divorced persons, the national rate is 39.9, including the extremely high rate of 69.4 for divorced males, as contrasted to 18.4 for divorced females.[16] For all age groups, except the fifteen to nineteen year olds and the eighty years and over groups, which have higher incidence, married persons have lower suicide rates than the single, widowed, or divorced (see Figure 1 for 1959 to 1961 three year average).

Specific factors of a general nature having a considerable bearing on suicide occurrence in all walks of life are delineated in the following descriptive categories.

Age

In more than half of all suicides, the age of the victim is forty-five years or more.[17] The aged person who finds himself alone, of no use now, unable to influence people as he used to, and whose relatives and friends have preceded him in death, is a most serious suicide risk. According to *Vital Health Statistics*

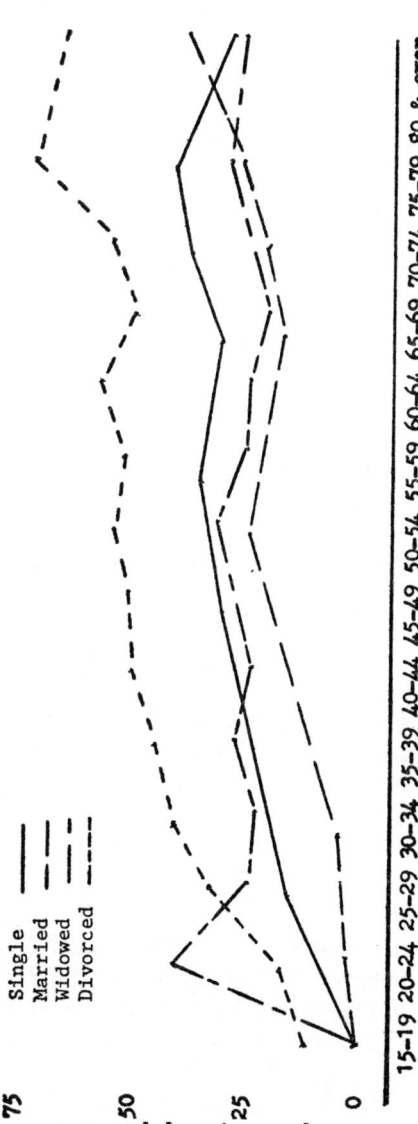

FIGURE 1.—Suicide rates by marital status and age: 1959-61 (3 year average)a

aMassey, "Suicide in the United States," p.7.

for 1950 through 1964, suicide rates for the United States increased with age at least until the 65-74 age group in some years and until the 75 and above age groups in other years.[18]

Suicide is rare in children under five years of age, though preoccupation with suicidal ideas can be common; and any actual occurrence is usually associated with violent, acting-out behavior.[19] Suicide is again rare in early adolescence; and when it does occur, there may be little indication of such severe disturbance.[20] Among young adults and college students, suicide is more common and ranks second after accidents as the leading cause of death.[21] Situational stresses accompanied by uncontrolled impulses seem to be especially dominant in this age group. For middle-aged and older adults suicide becomes much more lethal in terms of total numbers resorting to it.[22] Though it is interesting to note the decline of occurrence for this age group in recent years (see Figure 2, for suicide rates by age: 1950-1969).

The evidence of Figure 2 supports the conclusion offered by those who've said the trend in the age level of suicides is downward, implying that people are ending their own lives at an earlier and earlier age, while the number of suicides grow. Even so, advanced age still remains among the most immediate and significant factors in judging suicide potential.

It is important to notice the difference between suicide and attempted suicide in terms of ages when each occurs. Attempted suicide is most common in the teens and twenties, while suicide is most commonly found after age thirty. Shneidman and Farberow document this with their findings in research conducted at the Los Angeles Suicide Prevention Center.[23] They discovered in a study of 5,906 attempts and 768 committed suicides that both male and female commits show a modal age of forty-two, whereas among the attempted suicides the peak occurs at age thirty-two for males and twenty-seven for females. For both sexes, attempts in the sixties and above are relatively rare compared with commits (6 versus 27 per cent). There are more attempts among both sexes in their twenties and thirties than there are commits (56 versus 29 per cent).

Thus one may say the death rate from suicide increases with age, certainly in the United States and throughout most of the world, while suicide attempt rates tend to be highest among young

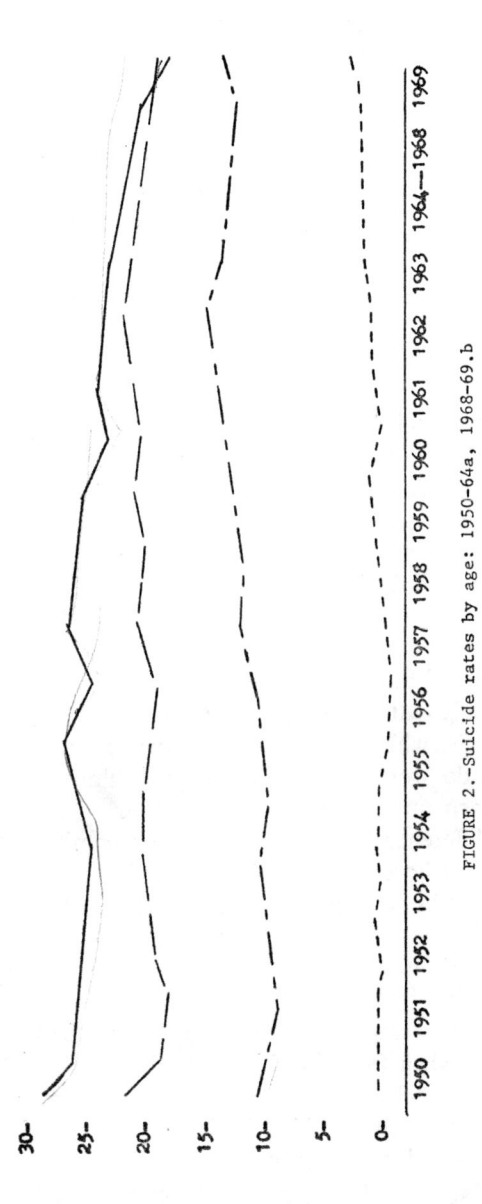

65 years and over ———
45-64 years — — —
25-44 years —··—··—
Under 25 years -------

FIGURE 2.—Suicide rates by age: 1950-64a, 1968-69.b

aMassey, "Suicide in the United States," p. 15.
bNational Center for Health Statistics, Mortality Statistics Branch (provisional figures).

and middle-adult ages. The tendency to earlier years in both categories is viewed with great concern.

Sex

Men kill themselves far more frequently than do women. The suicide rate for males in the United States averages 16 to 17 per 100,000 with the female rate at about 4 to 5 per 100,000 annually.[24] In 1964, seventy-three per cent of the persons committing suicide in the United States were males. In 1950 this percentage was seventy-eight.[25] This is commonly interpreted as, "three, or sometimes four times as many men kill themselves as do women."

Farberow and Shneidman state, "We have rarely encountered a nonlethally intended suicidal action in a man over fifty."[26] An emergency condition is considered to exist when a man over forty threatens suicide. Statistics generally support this level of serious occurrence for males around the world.

While men kill themselves more often, women attempt to do so more frequently. In fact, the percentages are almost the same for women attempting suicide as they are for men committing it. Shneidman and Farberow again indicate 70 per cent of the persons unsuccessfully attempting suicide in their 1957 study were females.[27] So while three or four times as many men commit suicide as do women, it's also true that three or four times as many women attempt suicide as do men.

This difference between men, who commit the suicidal act, and women, who generally only attempt it, will have far reaching consequences in other portions of our study. Initially, the obvious difference is that men who carry out suicidal acts generally intend to destroy themselves, while women have something other than self-destruction in mind.

A notable exception to the pattern occurs, however, during adolescence when for a brief time death by suicide is more common among females than males.[28] One could well wonder whether these were actually suicides in intent, or whether "accidents" during attempted suicide brought about fatalities.

Shneidman and Farberow point out an area for sensitive understanding of differences. They refer to statistics which indicate

Occurrence Factors

that as high as 80 per cent of the persons who commit suicide have previously attempted it.[29] If this is so, it indicates how an apparent difference must exist between the percentage of males who attempt and subsequently commit suicide and the percentage of females who do so.

Race

The rate of suicide and apparent risk of suicide varies considerably with different races. In general, the white population incurs a much greater suicide rate than the nonwhite races. In the United States suicide rates are approximately three times higher for whites than Negroes.[30] However, indications are that Negro rates are on the increase and at nearly an alarming pace in certain age groups. In fact, Herbert Hendin indicates that suicide is twice as frequent among New York Negro men between the ages of 20 and 35 as it is among white men of the same age group.[31] This and similar findings are leading authorities to conclude that black young adult males have the most rapidly increasing suicide rate in America today.

Other nonwhites, besides Negroes, have suicide rates very close to the Negro rate, thereby causing the overall ratio between rates for whites and nonwhite persons to be about two to one.[32] Suicide rates by race as recorded in *Vital Health Statistics* may be found in Table 2.

TABLE 2

Suicide Rates By Race
United States, 1960*, 1969†

Race	Both Sexes	Male	Female
		rate per 100,000 population	
All races†	10.9	15.7	6.4
White†	11.7	16.7	7.0
Negro*	3.9	6.4	1.6
Nonwhite†	5.0	8.0	2.3

*Massey, "Suicide in the United States," p. 5.
†National Center for Health Statistics, Mortality Statistics Branch, Rockville, Md. (Provisional figures.)

Researchers have also provided us the interesting indication that suicide rates among foreign born are higher than those of the native born, with the rates tending to be comparable to those of the country of origin.[33] While considerable research and attention is presently being devoted to the cause of difference in suicide rates among the races, the latter information tends to confirm thoughts regarding different influences of culture, environment, and identity group.

In their Los Angeles County study for 1957, Shneidman and Farberow offered statistics generally supporting the national rates for white-nonwhite suicide ratios. However, they also provided interesting evidence to the effect that there are proportionately more Negroes who attempt suicide than commit it (8 versus 3 per cent).[34] Unfortunately, limited information is available on this factor; but it will no doubt be receiving increased attention among all nonwhite studies and ratings.

Religion

The religious factor in suicide and attempted suicide is not altogether as simple or clear a matter as some statistical presentations would imply. There are some strong indications in certain directions, but nearly all these are matched by exceptions for which only partial answers are available.

In general, the consensus is that suicide rates are highest among Protestants, much lower among Catholics, and very much lower among Jews and Moslems.[35] Table 3 lists significant Protestant-Catholic ratings in countries with both predominant patterns and their exceptions.[36]

From Durkheim's early work to the present, religion has been considered as possibly among the antisuicidal forces. The question has remained, however, as to just how this is so and why the exceptions.

Most studies have been based upon simply identifying the particular faith to which one belonged. Very little has been done to explore the quality of dynamics of one's faith at work in his life. When one asks another if he is Catholic, for instance, does one mean: Were his parents? Was he baptized a Catholic? Is he currently attending Mass and Confession? or Does he have questions and doubt about his belief?

TABLE 3

Religious Preference and Suicide Rates: 1960*, 1967†‡

Predominantly Catholic: Low Rates		Catholic "Exceptions:" High Rates	
Irish Free State	3.0 (1960)	Austria	22.4
Spain	4.3	France	15.5
Italy	5.2	Hungary	31.3
Greece	3.4†		

Predominantly Protestant: High Rates		Protestant "Exceptions:" Low Rates	
West Germany	21.3	Northern Ireland	4.4 (1960)
West Berlin	40.9	Norway	7.0
Sweden	21.6	Netherlands	6.2
Denmark	17.5		
	(United States: 10.8)		

*Whalley, "Religion and Suicide," p. 14.
†The doctrinal position of the Greek Catholic Church resembles that of the Roman Catholic.
‡Lumen H. Long, ed., *The World Almanac* (New York: Newspaper Enterprise Assoc., Inc., 1971), p. 76. By permission.

The basic strength of religious influences in regard to suicide has been considered to be its cohesive, social solidifying characteristic. Thus Catholicism, with its clearer structure, has been evidenced as providing more social support. The exceptions challenging this generalization may be explained in part by special situations. Dublin feels, for instance, that the high rates in Hungary and West Berlin reflect the "turmoil incident to their exposure to communism."[37] Others would point to distinct social, economic, or political circumstances in describing exceptions.

Some researchers have realized the need of comparing countries of like factors, except religion. The United States and Canada would be good choices except that their official death certificates don't ask for religious affiliation. Where such studies have been conducted in Europe, Dublin says:

In all these countries the Protestants have shown uniformly higher rates than the Catholics, in many cases twice as high. . . . In general we find that suicide mortality is lowest in countries where a large proportion of the population is Catholic. Moreover, the suicide rate among Catholics is much lower than among Protestants living in the same country. . . .[38]

While Jewish rates of suicide have varied in different countries through various periods of history, generally they represent a lower rate. Israel's rates were reported as 8 per 100,000 in 1952 and 10 per 100,000 in 1958.[39]

Religion does appear to most researchers, therefore, to be a most significant factor in affecting suicide rates, not only because of specific religious prohibitions by certain faiths, but also, and primarily, because of the integration factors in society. Protestantism with individual emphasis and less forceful ecclesiastical pronouncements, thus appears to generally experience higher suicide rates than Catholics, Jews, Moslems, or other more structured and socially supportive faiths.

From previous sections of descriptive categories, we begin to see a predictable pattern of risk potential in suicide occurrence. A fifty year old male Caucasian, of Protestant faith, who talks about possibly committing suicide is to be considered a very high risk—especially if he should be of the medical profession, have a record of previous suicide attempt or have a history of mental illness. It should be noted that the majority of military personnel are male, Caucasian, and Protestant. Only age would be initially in their favor.

STATISTICAL INFORMATION

Before turning to actual statistics of occurrence, it would be helpful to be aware of certain variables which have been important in the study of suicide. Season variation is one such factor. Research has rather clearly indicated that suicides are more frequent in spring, with March, April, and May having the highest daily averages (see Figure 3).[40] April had the highest daily

Occurrence Factors

average in 10 of the 15 years from 1950 through 1964, May and June the highest for 2 years, and March for 1 year. A subsidiary peak may be observed in the month of October. The months with the lowest number of suicides per day are the winter months —November, December, and January.[41] No one is certain why the seasonal pattern is the way it is or why April is the cruelest month. The most common hypothesis is that someone who is depressed feels lonelier and more out of things than ever, when the rest of the world is enjoying spring. The same hypothesis might be extended to include what some have pointed out as an increase of suicides on key holidays such as Christmas or New Year's Eve.

Number of Suicides

FIGURE 3.—The Seasonal Patterns of Suicidal Deaths, 1964

The very day on which suicide occurs is a variable with interesting aspects as well. While occurrence of suicide may take place any time, of course, still indications are that certain days of the week are most often selected for the act. And, it should be pointed out, a different time of the week is apparently most often related to attempts. Pokorny's research demonstrates this from a three-year study in Houston (Table 4). He shows, in agreement with others, that suicide is a mid-week phenomenon with the peak day on Thursday, while attempted suicide most often occurs on a weekend with the peak on Sunday. Little information is available to explain this, yet the tendency is to say suicide is an action-type deed which occurs in the more active times of one's week.

TABLE 4

Distribution of Suicide and Attempted Suicide
Through Days of the Week*

Day of Week	Suicide (1960-1962)	Attempted Suicide (1961-1962)
Sunday	35	206
Monday	36	174
Tuesday	45	167
Wednesday	46	151
Thursday	48	139
Friday	31	148
Saturday	31	178

*Pokorny, "Human Violence: A Comparison of Homicide, Aggravated Assault, Suicide, and Attempted Suicide," p. 493.

The time of day also shows a specific relationship to suicide occurrence. Once more the active factor appears most important. Contrasted to homicides, suicide most often occurs in the daylight hours. Ten to 11 A.M. and 2 to 7 P.M. are the prime hours for suicides.[42] Attempted suicide, again reflecting perhaps less intensity, is reported to have peak hours in the after-work period of the day.

Weather has been another factor which people have wondered about in relationship to suicide occurrence. Pokorny, Davis, and Harberson have completed some extensive studies in this area which dealt with the eleven weather variables of temperature, wind speed, wind direction, barometric pressure, relative humidity, visibility, ceiling height, rain, fog, thunderstorms, and cloudiness. They concluded that "no single significant relationship was found." It is concluded that suicide and suicide attempts are not significantly related to weather phenomena.[43] The same basic conclusion was reached by Pokorny in regard to sunspots and moon phases.

Occurrence Factors

The place of occurrence is the final of these preliminary variables related to suicide. Both suicide and attempted suicide occur typically at home, again as contrasted to homicide which more typically occurs away from home. Suicide is a "private affair," with attempted suicide in this case appearing much the same. Pokorny's tabulation of 120 census tracts in Houston in 1960 indicates the private nature of suicidal acts in that the more private room, the bedroom, was most frequently chosen (Table 5).

TABLE 5

Place of Occurrence of Suicides
and Attempted Suicides
(In per cent)*

	Suicides (1960 only)	Attempted Suicide
Total Number of Cases	91	400
Bedroom	30.7	12.0
Living or Dining Room	12.1	1.8
Kitchen	7.7	3.0
Bathroom	8.8	9.2
Porch or Yard	2.2	0.7
Other Area of Home	9.9	1.8
Home, Area Unknown	4.4	50.7
Total at Home	75.8	79.2
Club, Bar, Lounge	0.0	0.7
Sidewalk, Parking Lot	0.0	0.0
Street, Alley	0.0	0.3
Car Away from Home	6.6	1.5
Other Areas Away from Home	15.4	18.3
Total, Away from Home	22.0	20.8
Unknown	2.2	0.0

*Pokorny, "Human Violence: A Comparison of Homicide, Aggravated Assault, Suicide, and Attempted Suicide," p. 491.

From the previous section and this one we can thus conclude that suicide and attempted suicide are similar in place, race, and ethnic grouping, but different in hour, day, age, and sex. The actual statistical occurrence of the phenomena of suicidal behavior will now receive our attention.

World Wide

Each day, an average of about 1,000 people in the world take their own lives and at least eight times this number attempt to do so, according to a report by the World Health Organization.[44] In most European countries and North America, suicide ranks among the first five to ten causes of death.

In a select number of countries picked by World Health Statistics, suicide ranked third, fourth, or fifth in causes of death for persons aged fifteen to forty-four years.[45] Suicide was one of the ten leading causes of death for persons of this age group (fifteen to forty-four) in ten out of seventeen countries in Africa, South and Central America, and Asia.

Countries with consistently low rates of suicide include: Mexico, Greece, Ireland, Spain, Italy and Israel. Countries with high rates are: Hungary, Austria, Sweden, West Germany, Japan, Denmark, Switzerland, and France. Both Canada and the United States have consistently been in the middle range.[46] Table 6 gives an indication of some significant worldwide rates.

TABLE 6

Suicides in Selected Countries†

1967 High rates	Rates per 100,000	Total Deaths Total	Male	Female
West Berlin	40.9	889	512	377
Hungary	31.3	3200	2227	973
Austria	22.4	1640	1117	523
Czechoslovakia	23.0*	3415	2427	988
Sweden	21.6	1702	1254	448
Germany (Fed. Republic)	21.3	12743	8373	4370
Finland*	19.2	933	729	204

Occurrence Factors

1967 High rates	Rates per 100,000	Total Deaths Total	Male	Female
Switzerland	18.4	1053	774	279
Denmark	17.5	847	565	282
France	15.5	7716	5683	2033
Australia	15.1	1778	1125	653
Belgium*	14.4	1434	980	454
Japan	13.9	14121	7940	6181
China-Taiwan	13.7	1805	1133	672
Medium rates				
United States	10.8	21325	15187	6138
Bulgaria	10.3	857	608	249
Poland	10.2	3268	2679	589
Hong Kong	10.1	388	239	149
New Zealand	10.0	274	191	83
England & Wales	9.7	4711	2736	1975
Portugal	9.6	906	706	200
Canada	9.0	1841	1353	488
Chile	7.6	696	525	171
Scotland	7.5	391	247	144
Norway	7.0	265	199	66
Low rates				
Israel	6.9	164	105	59
Colombia	6.5	1244	754	490
Netherlands	6.2	784	498	286
Italy	5.2	2913	2045	868
Spain	4.3	1442	1057	385
Greece	3.4	297	200	97
Ireland	2.5	72	54	18
Mexico	1.9	890	653	237

*1966

†Luman H. Long, ed., *The World Almanac* (New York: Newspaper Enterprise Assoc., Inc., 1971), p. 76.

When compared to previous years' records, these figures represent an increase in most countries from five to fifty per cent. Austria, since 1952-53, has gone up 56 per cent, Poland 50 per cent, Hungary 29 per cent, while Japan and Italy have each dropped 20 per cent in the same period.[47]

The general impression is one of an increase in most countries. The most striking feature of this increase has been the upswing in suicide among young persons, which is also reflected in the United States figures of recent years.

United States

With over 22,000 recorded deaths by suicide each year in the United States and an estimated unrecorded total of 75,000 to 100,000, suicide remains among the top eleven causes of death in this country.[48] And as previously indicated, suicide attempts range in estimated number of from five to nine for every suicide. The extent of occurrence immediately becomes dramatic as well as a source of great concern. Cause-of-death statistics for 1964 show an average of 56 suicides committed daily in the United States. Suicide has been among the twelve leading causes of death for the past ten years.[49] It has been even more prominent among teenagers and young adults. It ranked fourth in 1964 for age groups fifteen to twenty-four and twenty-five to forty-four years.

Table 7 indicates the rates for nineteen years by age and sex per 100,000 population. Note the higher rates for the last few years, higher male than female and higher white than nonwhite rates (page 35).

The increased total occurrence rates of the last few years (1962 to 1969) can be understood by studying Table 8 (page 36) which lists the same years by age groups. It can be seen how decreased occurrence in later years is more than made up for by the increase during young adult years.

Table 9, which indicates geographical distribution of suicide by areas in the United States, shows the problem as most pronounced in the West, particularly along the West Coast. Movement and accompanying lack of social integration are generally offered as possible explanations (page 37).

The ranking of cities by suicide rates confirms the West Coast figures of high occurrence with San Francisco-Oakland, California, having a rate of 17.2 and Los Angeles-Long Beach, California, having a rate of 17.1 per 100,000. Tampa-St. Petersburg, Florida, is credited with its high rating (17.3 per 100,000), because of the large, older age retirement population. Cities having medium

TABLE 7

Age-Adjusted Suicide Rates, by Color and Sex:
United States, 1950-1964* and 1967-1969†

Year	Total Both Sexes	Total Male	Total Female	White Both Sexes	White Male	White Female	Nonwhite Both Sexes	Nonwhite Male	Nonwhite Female
1969	10.9	15.7	6.4	11.7	16.7	7.0	5.0	8.0	2.3
1968	10.7	15.8	5.9	11.5	16.9	6.3	4.8	7.3	2.4
1967	10.8	15.7	6.1	11.6	16.8	6.5	5.0	7.6	2.7
1964	11.0	16.6	5.8	11.6	17.4	6.2	5.7	9.1	2.6
1963	11.3	17.0	6.0	11.9	17.9	6.4	6.1	9.9	2.7
1962	11.0	16.8	5.6	11.7	17.9	6.0	5.7	9.0	2.7
1961	10.5	16.4	5.0	10.9	17.1	5.3	5.7	9.5	2.2
1960	10.6	16.6	5.0	11.1	17.5	5.3	5.4	8.7	2.3
1959	10.5	16.6	4.7	11.0	17.4	4.9	5.5	9.1	2.3
1958	10.5	16.8	4.7	11.1	17.6	5.0	5.1	8.4	2.1
1957	9.6	15.3	4.2	10.0	16.0	4.5	4.7	8.1	1.6
1956	9.7	15.5	4.4	10.3	16.3	4.6	4.4	7.1	1.8
1955	9.9	15.7	4.5	10.4	16.5	4.8	4.3	7.1	1.7
1954	9.9	16.0	4.1	10.4	16.8	4.3	4.6	7.8	1.7
1953	9.8	15.7	4.2	10.3	16.5	4.5	4.3	7.3	1.4
1952	9.7	15.3	4.3	10.2	16.1	4.6	4.1	6.9	1.4
1951	10.0	15.8	4.6	10.5	16.5	4.8	4.5	7.3	1.9
1950	11.0	17.3	4.9	11.6	18.1	5.3	4.8	7.8	1.8

*Massey, "Suicide in the United States," p. 14.
†National Center for Health Statistics, General Mortality, Vol. II, 1968, Section I.

TABLE 8

Suicide Rates by Age: United States, 1950-64,* 1968-72†

Year	All ages	5-14 years	15-24 years	25-34 years	35-44 years	45-54 years	55-64 years	65-74 years	75-84 years	85 years and over
1972	11.7	0.1	9.7	14.3	16.7	19.7	20.5	20.3	20.4	18.5
1971	11.1	0.3	9.2	13.2	16.0	18.8	19.2	22.0	20.3	17.7
1970	11.1	0.3	9.2	14.2	14.7	20.1	19.9	20.3	18.4	—
1969	11.1	0.3	7.8	13.4	16.5	18.3	22.4	19.4	21.4	15.5
1968	10.7	0.3	7.1	12.1	16.2	19.6	21.8	19.6	20.8	22.1
1964	10.8	0.2	6.0	11.9	15.6	20.5	22.7	22.1	23.9	25.3
1963	11.0	0.3	6.0	11.8	16.0	21.1	23.6	22.4	25.4	24.6
1962	10.9	0.3	5.7	11.3	15.0	21.0	23.7	22.2	27.2	26.7
1961	10.4	0.2	5.1	10.3	14.4	20.3	23.1	22.0	26.0	24.9
1960	10.6	0.3	5.2	10.0	14.2	20.7	23.7	23.0	27.9	26.0
1959	10.6	0.2	4.9	9.9	13.6	19.8	24.3	24.8	27.8	25.7
1958	10.7	0.2	4.8	9.8	13.7	20.7	24.1	25.1	27.7	25.8
1957	9.8	0.2	4.0	8.7	12.7	18.2	22.4	23.6	26.5	26.4
1956	10.0	0.2	4.0	8.5	12.1	18.5	24.2	25.2	28.0	23.5
1955	10.2	0.1	4.1	8.4	12.3	19.6	24.8	25.0	27.5	27.9
1954	10.1	0.1	4.2	8.7	12.5	19.3	23.9	25.1	25.6	25.1
1953	10.1	0.2	4.4	8.5	12.6	18.7	22.4	25.5	28.0	27.9
1952	10.0	0.2	4.2	8.5	12.6	18.3	22.5	25.6	27.9	31.2
1951	10.4	0.2	4.4	8.6	13.3	18.8	23.2	27.1	27.7	30.5
1950	11.4	0.2	4.5	9.1	14.3	20.9	26.8	29.6	31.1	28.8

*Massey, "Suicide in the United States," p. 15.
†National Center for Health Statistics, Mortality Statistics Branch, Vital Statistics Reports, 1971-72.

rates are New York, and Washington, D.C.-Suburban Maryland-Virginia. Lower rates are found in Dallas, Texas, 7.9 per 100,000, Newark, New Jersey, 6.9 per 100,000, and Providence, Rhode Island, 6.7 per 100,000.[50]

TABLE 9

Suicide Rates for United States
By Geographic Division
1967*

Area	Total
United States (Total)	10.8
New England	8.8
Middle Atlantic	8.0
East North Central	10.3
West North Central	10.9
South Atlantic	10.8
East South Central	9.5
West South Central	9.4
Mountain	14.6
Pacific	17.1

1967 Vital Statistics of the United States, Vol. 11, Mortality.

Young Adults

Around the world, concern is increasing over the rise of suicide rates among the younger population. More countries are beginning to resemble Japan's suicide structure which reaches a peak at the ages of twenty to twenty-five with 15.1 per cent of all deaths in that age group resulting from suicide. Some have passed Japan, such as West Berlin, with 37.2 per cent, Czechoslovakia—17.5 per cent, and Hungary—24.9 per cent. The United States rate is 6.0 per cent for this age group, with the peak occurrence in the twenty-five to thirty-four age group at 8.0 per cent.[51]

While the suicide rate among older persons in the United States has been declining since the 1930's, the suicide rate among young people has been rising. Since 1950, suicide among youth aged fifteen to twenty-four has climbed from the fifth ranking cause of death to the third. In 1966, it has been estimated that nearly 100,000 college students threatened suicide; of these, one in ten actually attempted suicide and 1,000 completed the act.[52]

Among college students, suicide is the second greatest cause of death, while accidents, the first cause, may also actually contain additional suicides. For students, the rate of suicide is 50 per cent higher than for other Americans of comparable age.[53] They are the highest potential suicide risk group. Suicide is reported to have been responsible for as many as 50 per cent of student deaths at the University of Michigan in 1934, 34 per cent at the University of California at Berkeley in 1965, 27 per cent at Oxford in 1959, and 15 per cent at Harvard in 1961.[54] In 1967 the college population suicide rate was determined to be 15.0 per 100,000.[55]

Despite what many feel to be increased social stigma attached to this age group with the shame and guilt it brings to friends and relatives, still a 25 per cent increase in reported suicide attempts has occurred among persons under twenty years of age in the past decade.[56] The number of completions has nearly doubled.

Table 10 gives the rates for ages fifteen to twenty-four from 1955 to 1972, which indicates over 100.57 per cent increase in that age group.[57]

Armed Forces

Suicide has been a great problem throughout the years in the armed forces. Rates of occurrence have fluctuated greatly from one period to another. Lack of reports and reports as accidents have made it very difficult to obtain accurate information. Dr. Hauschild, for example, tells of the young soldier who ran ahead of his group, disrobing as he went. He then jumped into a swift-flowing river and swam to the middle where he remained despite cries from his associates. Finally, he disappeared. This was officially ruled "accidental drowning."[58]

In examining rates of previous decades, one becomes aware of how serious the problem of suicide has been to the armed forces. In 1903 the suicide rate of various armies recorded per 100,000: 18 in France, 24 in Italy, 36 in Germany, 105 in

TABLE 10
Suicide Rates: 15-24 Years*†

Year	Total	Male	Female
1972	9.7		
1971	9.2		
1970	9.2		
1968	7.1	10.9	3.4
1964	6.0	9.2	2.8
1963	6.0	9.0	3.1
1962	5.7	8.5	2.9
1961	5.1	7.9	2.3
1960	5.2	8.2	2.2
1959	4.9	7.7	2.1
1958	4.8	7.4	2.3
1957	4.0	6.4	1.8
1956	4.0	6.3	1.9
1955	4.1	6.3	2.0

*Massey, "Suicide in the United States," p. 15.
†National Center for Health Statistics, Mortality Statistics Branch (Provisional Figures).

Austria, and 133 in Russia.[59] The highest frequency from this study was noted in the cavalry, while rates declined in the infantry and artillery, and were much lower in the engineering troops.

Engelstad has quoted a number of studies which show that suicide was the main reason of death in the U.S. Army during the years before World War II.[60] Some figures are quoted of suicides in the U.S. Navy for years during the same period ranging from 21 to 26 per 100,000 (more than double the present U.S. male young adult rate). These rates reportedly dropped to 14 per 100,000 during the first year of the war.

An exhaustive study of 656 homicides and 1179 suicides which covered the entire U.S. Army in all theaters of operation during World War II was compiled by Zamcheck and Geisler. Of all cases involving suicide, 339 or 28.8 per cent were in the 18 to 24 age group with an age-specific rate of occurrence of 5.6

per 100,000.[61] This rate was lower for suicides among young adult deaths than either before the war or in subsequent years of peace, including the present. Another finding of their study, which is apparently not typical today, indicated that suicides among officers was more than twice as high as that among enlisted men in both World War I and World War II. Furthermore, the Medical Department comprising only 6 per cent of the total military personnel contributed more than 10 per cent of the suicides. Suicides were most frequent in the morning between the hours of five and ten, reaching the peak between 7 and 9 A.M. Suicides occurred twice as frequently as homicide. Negroes committed suicide far less frequently than one would expect for their total number (nonwhite specific rate—2.8). Chances were five to one that a Negro soldier dead from unnatural causes was a victim of homicide rather than suicide. On the other hand, chances were three to one that a white soldier in similar circumstances was a suicide.

Present suicide rates in the armed forces, from available statistics, appear to run below the comparable rates for males across the U.S. civilian society. However, it is most difficult to verify this exactly, as comparable age groups are not divided the same in suicide ratings. The civilian male, fifteen to twenty-four age group (9.2), would be too low a figure to compare with military figures which would begin at age seventeen. The two younger years would tend to lower the civilian average. Some figures from civilian ratings are available for the twenty to twenty-four age group (14.9), but this would be too high compared to military rates, as the seventeen to nineteen year olds would lower a seventeen to twenty-four age military figure. Perhaps a rough splitting of difference at about 11 or 11.5 would be the civilian rate for comparison. Even this would not be equitable as most military rates include all ages. While the majority of military are young adults, higher rates for older men would tend to raise their figures slightly. Therefore, it might be said that any military figure under 11 or 12 per 100,000 will compare favorably with comparable U.S. civilian figures.

Navy and Marine Corps rates per 100,000 for the latest years available as provided by the Office of the Surgeon General are: 1966—8.7, 1967—10.2, 1968—10.9.[62] These figures are based upon ninety, one hundred and six, and one hundred and seventeen deaths by suicide in those respective years. It is interesting, however, to note a study by Colonel Eggertsen, Chief of Psychiatry at Travis Air Force Base, California, who gives a suicide average in the Air Force from 1958 to 1964 as 11.9 per 100,000.[63] This figure would bring military rates more on a par with our estimated comparable civilian figure. The Army Surgeon General's Office reports rates of 13.3, 10.4, and 10.2 per 100,000 for 1965, 1966, and 1967. These figures represent one hundred twenty-nine, one hundred twenty-six, and one hundred forty-six deaths by suicide for the respective years.[64] The latter, again, would indicate military rates as possibly somewhat below comparable civilian figures for suicide occurrence.

Yet, another study would indicate that suicide *attempts* are more common in the military than in civilian life. Tucker and Reinhardt report that one out of five psychiatric patients whom a military physician sees will have a suicidal component to his problem.[65] This is explained by referring to the suicidal gesture as a dramatic mode of communication by which the young military man most often says, "Please help me get out of the service, I can't stand it any more." The one out of five or 20 per cent cited in this study is actually much lower than reports from San Diego and Oakland Naval Hospitals which for 1964 and 1965 indicated 36 and 23.4 per cent respectively as the number of suicidal tendency patients among all other psychiatric patients.[66]

The results of one study rather surprisingly say that within a particular suicide group, "the frequency of attempts was higher among enlistees (1 per 3.5) than among draftees (1 per 5.7)."[67]

In support of general public findings, there is some indication that military suicide rates are reaching their peak at younger ages. In three recent years, Air Force personnel under twenty years of age exhibited a higher suicide rate than those in the twenty to twenty-four age group.[68]

An encouraging note also is sounded by some findings which indicate that military suicide rates are tending to hold steady as compared to the rising civilian population rates.[69] This is generally thought to be because of the "screening effect" on those coming into the military, by which younger, healthier, more intelligent and a little more successful group of people are admitted. The readily available facilities for personal care along with organized, structured life seem to also be significant factors.

NOTES

1. Edwin S. Shneidman and David D. Swenson, eds., "Suicide Among Youth," *Bulletin of National Institute of Mental Health* (December, 1969), p. 4.
2. Stanley F. Yolles, *The Tradgedy of Suicide in the U.S.* (Chevy Chase, Md.: National Institute of Mental Health, 1965), p. 1.
3. *Ibid.*
4. Berblinger, "Suicide as a Message," p. 144.
5. James T. Massey, "Suicide in the United States," *Vital Health Statistics*, XX (August, 1967), p. 1.
6. Louis I. Dublin, *Factbook on Man From Birth to Death* (New York: The Macmillan Company, 1965), p. 261.
7. Stengel, *Suicide and Attempted Suicide*, p. 11.
8. *Ibid.*, p. 12.
9. Dublin, *Factbook on Man From Birth to Death*, p. 263.
10. *Ibid.*, p. 265.
11. Roche Laboratories, *Suicide Prevention: The Burden of Responsibility*, p. 16.
12. *Ibid.*
13. Bruyn and Seiden, "Student Suicide: Fact or Fancy," p. 70.
14. "Ways to Prevent Suicide," *Nature*, CCXX (November, 1968), p. 418.
15. *Ibid.*
16. Yolles, *The Tragedy of Suicide in the U.S.*, p. 5.
17. Iver F. Small and Murray M. De Armond, "Clinical Assessment and Management of the Potential Suicide," *Journal of the Indiana State Medical Association*, LIX (November, 1966), p. 1302.
18. Massey, "Suicide in the United States," p. 4.
19. Bosselman, *Self-Destruction*, p. 12.
20. Small and De Armond, "The Clinical Assessment and Management of the Potential Suicide," p. 1301.
21. *Ibid.*, p. 1302.
22. Morhauser, "Suicide," p. 2.
23. Norman L. Farberow and Edwin S. Shneidman, eds., *The Cry for Help* (New York: McGraw-Hill Book Company, 1965), p. 28.
24. Roche Laboratories, *Suicide Prevention: The Burden of Responsibility*, p. 8.
25. Massey, "Suicide in the United States," p. 5.
26. Small and DeArmond, "The Clinical Assessment and Management of the Potential Suicide," p. 1302.
27. Roche Laboratories, *Suicide Prevention: The Burden of Responsibility*, p. 8.

Occurrence Factors

28. Small and De Armond, "The Clinical Assessment and Management of the Potential Suicide," p. 1302.
29. Farberow and Shneidman, *The Cry For Help*, p. 28.
30. Small and De Armond, "The Clinical Assessment and Management of the Potential Suicide," p. 1302.
31. Herbert Hendin, "Black Suicide," *Archives of General Psychiatry*, XXI (October, 1969), p. 407.
32. Roche Laboratories, *Suicide Prevention: The Burden of Responsibility*, p. 10.
33. *Ibid.*, p. 11.
34. Farberow and Shneidman, *The Cry for Help*, p. 28.
35. Small and De Armond, "The Clinical Assessment and Management of the Potential Suicide," p. 1302.
36. Whalley, "Religion and Suicide," p. 14.
37. Louis I. Dublin, *Suicide: A Sociological and Statistical Study* (New York: The Ronald Press, 1963), p. 75.
38. *Ibid.*, p. 78.
39. Whalley, "Religion and Suicide," p. 17.
40. Massey, "Suicide in the United States," p. 17.
41. Roche Laboratories, *Suicide Prevention: The Burden of Responsibility*, p. 13.
42. Jim Castelli, "Suicide—The Whispered Word," *The Catholic News* (New York), February 5, 1970, p. 1.
43. Alex D. Pokorny, Fred Davis, and Wayne Harberson, "Suicide, Suicide Attempts, and Weather," *The American Journal of Psychiatry*, CXX, No. 4 (October, 1963), p. 381.
44. "Ways to Prevent Suicide," p. 417.
45. "Mortality Statistics: Suicides," *World Health Statistics Report*, XXI, No. 6 (1968), p. 365.
46. Vincent, "Suicide and How to Prevent It," p. 346.
47. Shneidman and Swenson, eds., "Suicide Among Youth," p. 5.
48. Small and De Armond, "The Clinical Assessment and Management of the Potential Suicide," p. 1301.
49. Massey, "Suicide in the United States," p. 1.
50. *Ibid.*, p. 34.
51. "Mortality Statistics: Suicides," pp. 409-410.
52. Ross, "Suicide Among College Students," p. 106.
53. *Ibid.*
54. *Ibid.*
55. John M. Whiteley, "Student Stress, Suicide, and the Role of the University," *Journal of the National Association of Women Deans and Counselors*, XXX (Spring, 1967), p. 121.
56. Faigel, "Suicide Among Young Persons: A Review of its Incidence and Causes," p. 187.
57. "Sharp Rise in Deaths Among Young Men," Statistical Bulletin of Metropolitan Life of New York (August 1969), p. 8.

58. T. B. Hauschild, "Suicide in Europe," *Medical Bulletin U.S. Army Europe,* XXI (August, 1964), p. 250.

59. Ulf Otto, "Suicidal Attempts Made During Compulsory Military Service," *Acta Psychiatrica Scandinavica,* XXXIX (1963), p. 299.

60. J. Chr. Bull Engelstad, "Suicides and Attempted Suicides in the Norwegian Armed Forces During Peace Time," *Military Medicine,* CXXXIII (June, 1968), p. 438.

61. Norman Zamcheck and Murray A. Geisler, "Homicides and Suicides of World War II," *Journal of Forensic Science,* V (1960), p. 86.

62. Chief, Bureau of Medicine and Surgery Department of the Navy, "Death Tabulations," Washington, D.C., 23 November 1971.

63. P. F. Eggertsen and S. M. Goldstein, "Suicide by Air Force Personnel 1958 to 1964," *Military Medicine,* CXXXIII (January, 1968), p. 27.

64. Office of the Surgeon General Department of the Army, "Suicides and Suicide Rates: U.S. Army Male Personnel (1910-1967)", Washington, D.C., 18 November 1971.

65. Gary J. Tucker and Roger F. Reinhardt, "Suicide Attempts," Research conducted at Naval Aerospace Medical Institute, Pensacola, Florida (August 8, 1966), p. 11.

66. Navy Medical Neuropsychiatric Research Unit, "Percentages of Patient Groups with Suicidal Tendencies," San Diego, California, 1969. (Typewritten.)

67. William Offenkrantz, Edwin Church, and Robert Elliott, "Psychiatric Management of Suicide Problems in Military Service," *American Journal of Psychiatry,* CIXIV (1957), p. 40.

68. Eggertsen and Goldstein, "Suicide by Air Force Personnel 1958 to 1964," p. 29.

69. *Ibid.*, p. 27.

3. Causes, Dynamics and Motivations

CLASSICAL THEORIES

The first question asked by anyone knowing the person who committed suicide is, "Why do men kill themselves?" The deceased was most likely upset, but that in itself does not explain

Causes, Dynamics and Motivations

why he took his life. Others are upset, but they continue to live. What makes one different from another? Why do some give up? Suicide has puzzled mankind for centuries, and only in recent decades have men begun to make scientific sense of the puzzle.

The earliest theories of men regarding suicide and attempted suicide were largely "demonologic and theologic."[1] As has been previously cited, ancient taboos and Christian convictions against suicide placed it among the bizarre and socially unacceptable categories of sinful and criminal behavior. Most speculation and argument revolved around the right of the individual to take his own life. In the main, it could therefore be said that suicidal behavior was viewed as conscious and volitional.

With the dawn of the Enlightenment, men such as Donne, Hume, Hobbes, and Berkeley, among a host of others, called for a new understanding of suicide with emphasis upon individual rights, and study of the intriguing unknown and fanciful new beginnings it apparently offered.[2]

Not until the end of the nineteenth century, however, did the real breakthrough occur in understanding suicide. Durkheim's monumental work in 1897, which dealt with the forces of society upon the individual, launched anthropologists, sociologists, psychologists, psychiatrists and, most recently, semantic experts into a search of the dynamics involved in self-destructive behavior. While emphases have shifted from one stream of thought to another, as with the advancement of Freud's psychoanalytic theory, the increasing tendency is to see the need for a multi-faceted approach in understanding suicidal behavior.

Many like Kobler and Stotland have concluded that "Literature on depression in suicide does not indicate a distinct set of dynamics specifically toward suicide."[3] Others would heartily agree with Meerloo who calls for "an infinite number of motivations" in suicidal reactions.[4]

Yet, complex as suicide portends to be, one can be grateful for some specific avenues guiding our understanding. Before turning to the major theories explaining what suicide is, let us pause briefly to note what research has indicated it is not. To this date, at least, suicidal behavior is not considered to be biologically inherited or to run in families.[5] Suicide does not necessarily occur in overly disturbed or mentally ill persons, nor is it always the act of a psychotic person.[6] While there may be many indications of unhappiness by the suicidal, this is not to be equated with mental illness. Suicide is not necessarily a life-long threat to one who has once been suicidal.[7] In fact, individuals tend to be "suicidal" for only a limited period of time. Suicide is not prevented by good financial circumstances.[8] And, as indicated previously, it is not related to changes in climate, moon phases, or other cosmic factors, so far as research can determine.[9]

In turning to examine suicide theories, the psychoanalytic approach, though later evolving, shall be considered first since it has become most poignant in contemporary understanding. This approach deals with the problem as men very likely were most concerned with it through the ages—in light of what is happening within the particular suicidal individual.

Psychoanalytic

The most important psychological insight into suicide came from Sigmund Freud beginning with his writings on "Mourning and Melancholia" in 1916.[10] While the writing dealt primarily with depression, Freud was able to show how these dynamics fed into the experience of suicide. He explains the self-torments of melancholiacs as meeting a gratification of sadistic tendencies and of hate. Both of these, he says, relate to an object and have been turned around upon the self. "It is this sadism," he continues, "and only this, that solves the riddle of the tendency to suicide . . ."[11] The ego, he explains, which possesses such immense self love, can kill itself only when it can treat itself as an object, and launch itself against the animosity relating to an object of the outer world. The object is indeed abolished, but at cost of the self.

This theory has been described as aggression turned upon oneself. It is the same impulse as homicide, only in this case turned inward rather than outward. The action is based upon deep instinctive drives—*Eros* (life) and *Thanatos* (death)—which are in constant struggle within oneself. In a person who commits suicide, the death or self-destructive drive suddenly bursts its bounds, springs into power, and puts an immediate end to the existence of the individual.[12] Freud doubted that there would be a suicide without the repressed desire to kill someone else. While his later views brought an expansion to these original ideas, the basics are not to be forgotten—namely, that anger can become self-directed, can lead to depression, and can be a motivating force in suicide.

This led Anna Freud to conclude that adolescent suicide is expression of omnipotent behavior in the Oedipus conflict and symbolizes the destruction of the object which has been sado-masochistically invested and introjected.[13] She felt a grave emotional deprivation suffered in early childhood and relived in adolescence could be too severe a trauma and lead to suicide.

Perhaps best known in the suicide field from the contemporary period is Karl Menninger with his theories of the "three steps" and the "significant other." Expanding upon Freudian concepts, Menninger says that suicide is really a tripartite process involving the wish to kill, the wish to be killed, and the wish to die.[14] He feels that close scrutiny of the deeper motives for suicide would confirm there are regularly two of these elements and sometimes all three in effect. They combine, says Menninger, to impel with vectorial force the precipitate self-destruction.

Menninger says the wish to kill may begin with the first thwartings of life such as deprival of satisfactions in nursing. This brings out aggressive impulses that may in turn be followed by a long list of self directed aggressions. A boy killing himself after a quarrel with his father is killing the "introjected father."[15]

The wish to be killed is described as the supreme form of submission, just as killing is the extreme form of aggression. Menninger says this may take the form of trying to catch pneumonia or getting a heart attack in strenuous athletics.

The wish to die, while admittedly only a hypothesis compared to the previous two, may still be observed in daredevils and others convinced of desirability of death even if they can't bring themselves to carry it out.

An attempt at suicide is above all a desperate cry for life. Most suicides are seen as a "gamble" in which sufficient warning is given to allow the "significant others" to save the suicide's life.[16] Suicide attempts are thus above all a message of desperation. Menninger believes all we need to retain desire for life is one "significant other"; that is, a person who cares.

Otto Fenichel extends Freud's theory by adding elements of fear, guilt, and coercive rage to the motivating dynamic of suicide. These he describes as mixed in "an ambivalent dependence on a sadistic superego and the necessity to get rid of an unbearable guilt tension at any cost."[17] This becomes the most frequent cause of suicide, according to Fenichel. He says a mixture of submission and rebellion is the climax of efforts in coercing forgiveness. It's the—"Look what you have done to me."

Attempted suicide is analyzed by Fenichel as often connected with hopeful and pleasurable fantasies such as looking for union with mother or reconciliation by killing the punishing superego and regaining union with the protecting superego.[18]

Sandor Rado pursues this theme further in describing a depressive spell as a desperate cry for love precipitated by a real or imagined loss which endangers the patient's security.[19] Blame is placed upon self for the loss and reconciliation is attempted through the supreme sacrifice, which will secure the loved ones nourishing graces forever.

Zilboorg, Stone, Friedlander, Schmidsberg, Dorpat, Ripley, Lewin, Glover, and Hendin along with scores of others have followed psychoanalytic paths adding certain refinements and personal variations to basic themes emanating from Freud.

Nonpsychoanalytic

The really classical and first scientific work on suicide was in 1897 by the French sociologist Emile Durkheim titled simply *Le Suicide*. His approach to understanding suicide was based on the view which says the whole is greater than the sum of its parts. In contrast to the psychoanalytic view, which followed his, Durkheim insisted that suicide is "explicable etiologically with reference to the social structure, and its ramifying functions."[20] He saw suicide to be the result of society's strength or weakness of control over the individual.

According to Durkheim, three basic types of suicide may be found, depending upon man's relationship to his society. The first is *Egoistic* which implies that man seeks to kill himself because of a loss of cohesion in his society.[21] Excessive individualism springs from weakened groups and relationships causing the ego

Causes, Dynamics and Motivations

to assert itself even at the expense of its own life. When the individual has too few ties with his community, demands to live don't reach him. Strong church ties or family relationships thus tend to prevent suicide. The ties of security and solidarity in Roman Catholicism are cited at this point as reasons for lower suicide rates than in Protestantism.

The second type, *Altruistic* suicide, occurs, says Durkheim, when society holds the individual in too strict tutelage.[22] In other words, this is the very opposite of the egoistic type. The ego is not its own property, and may be called upon by society to sacrifice itself as in Indian suttee or Japanese hara-kiri. It should be noted that Durkheim later refers to this as the distinctive suicide form among military personnel. Not only are they disciplined to offer up their lives for the greater good of society, but Durkheim feels this reduction of individual life, as the ultimate value, sets up possibilities for easy sacrifice in a variety of stressful situations.[23]

Finally, Durkheim describes *Anomic* suicide as that voluntary death which occurs when crises or disturbances of equilibrium take place in the collective order.[24] This condition comes to pass when one's activities lack regulation or stability. It is akin to the egoistic suicide as both indicate the insufficient presence of society in individual life. Loss of a job, close friend, or fortune could result in anomic suicide.

In further writings, Durkheim classifies suicides of the insane as: (1) Maniacal, (2) Melancholy, (3) Obsessive, and (4) Impulsive or Automatic.[25] He also asserts that suicide can be very contagious, though not inherited. He feels individuals susceptible to suggestion, as in hypnosis, could become predisposed to the idea of self-destruction.

G. M. Davidson, proceeding in the nonpsychoanalytic approach to suicide, offered the theory that the person at the time of his suicidal attempt, has reached the limit of his resources and has lost his goal.[26]

Crichton-Miller attributes suicide to a failure of adaptation and looks upon it as final regression from reality.[27] Usually present, he says, are signs of social suffering, fears, doubts, dread, and pain.

Wiele suggested suicide varies according to area types with "tired of life" in advantaged suburbs and "emotional strains" in moderately advantaged suburbs; while in least advantaged areas reasons are hardly offered, only instructions as to dispensation of the corpse.[28]

Others like Teicher, Lewis, Clark, Henry, and Short have continued to advance Durkheim's basic sociological approach through studies of crises, social structures, and community effects in preventing or enhancing the probability of suicide.

SUBSEQUENT RESEARCH

This section will provide a five-directional exploration of some significant research and findings evolving from earlier classical theories regarding causes, dynamics, and motivations in suicide and attempted suicide.
The five areas will include:
(1) Theories by more recent writers in this field.
(2) Research on suicide in the general population.
(3) Findings pertaining to young people.
(4) Specific dynamics among college students.
(5) Research with young adults in the armed forces.

Among a host of scholars, researchers, and writers, who through the years have made notable contributions to the increased understanding of suicide, the following are highlighted as especially significant and pertinent to this study.

Carl Jung in his essay "The Soul and Death," says, "The negation of life's fulfillment is synonymous with the refusal to accept its ending."[29] Life must be meaningful with the ego and total self maintaining contact with the world, or life cannot be accepted. The darker side of the self, says Jung, may prevail causing the death of the ego that it may return to the womb to reestablish contact and be reborn.

The Adlerian theory of dynamics sees individuals as a unique whole, striving for a goal of success.[30] The individual influences society and in turn is influenced by it. All maladjustment, including suicide, is seen by Alfred Adler as a deficiency in social interest (capacity for harmony with self, others, and the world). Suicide tendencies develop with pampered life style, self-centered goals, and veiled aggression.

Harry Stack Sullivan has felt one must focus on the particular

Causes, Dynamics and Motivations

patterns of interaction between persons within a cultural milieu to understand suicide.[31] Suicide is that self-destructive activity resulting from hateful or hostile types of integration with others, which cannot be explained by a single theory.

Karen Horney sees suicide as a failure of development of the self or incomplete development, such as in alcoholics.[32] Horney, unlike Freud, would say man is not born with innate self-destructive tendencies. Suicide and neurosis spring from the same source, which is the self becoming a subordinated instrument dependent on outer forces for control.

Victor E. Frankl traces neuroses in general and suicide more particularly, to failure in finding meaning and responsibility in existence.[33] Man becomes frustrated in the will-to-meaning quest.

Louis I. Dublin comes close to Frankl in saying, suicide and homicide "both are reactions to frustrations generated sometimes by economic, sometimes by social forces, and often by forces within the individual himself."[34]

Erwin Stengel feels acts of self-damage are probably due to a combination of at least two tendencies, the urge to self-destruction and the urge to make others show concern and love.[35] This leads him to emphasize attempted suicide as a different behavior pattern from suicide, namely as alarm signals and appeals for help.

Norman Farberow and Edwin Shneidman have at the same time referred to all suicidal behavior as basically a "cry for help," which gives us clues for predictions and hope for prevention.[36]

James Hillman and George Kelly, working separately, have stimulated much thought by in part referring to suicide as the impulse to encounter absolute reality a "demand for fuller life through the death experience";[37] and as an act by which one may "sensibly endeavor to validate his reality."[38]

In development of suicide theory, one thus moves from self and society to interaction between the two, then to a search for meaningful values and acceptance in relationships, and finally to significant validation of life here and beyond this earthly existence.

Clinical research leading to additional findings and theories regarding the dynamics of suicide encompasses a vast amount of material. It shall be our purpose now to only touch lightly upon a few of the most pertinent findings.

Research has revealed that there is no one specific personality structure among the suicidal, but that suicide may be attempted when certain individuals suffer from a cluster of situational stresses beyond their coping ability. For this reason, suicide often occurs in responsible, religious, or "successful" families.[39] The occurrence may take place even as one plans for the future or prepares for a vacation. The experience of not enjoying even a vacation may be the "last straw."

While it has been already stated that suicide is not necessarily to be equated with mental illness, research has also indicated that it is not an indicator of good mental health either. Increasingly, it is being viewed as a hitherto unnamed psychic disease, only in the rarest cases a genuine mental illness, but rather a disturbance in mental balance brought about by unresolved conflicts.[40]

In such a state the person knows that he is doomed. Severe depression may set in as one realizes there are no choices, no way out, "no exit," only self-annihilation.[41] The individual may have drawn up a mental list of assets and liabilities and then given himself over to *Bilanz-Selbstmord*—balance sheet suicide.[42]

Death may be seen as retaliatory abandonment by which the victim gains illusory control over the situation, or it may be operating as retroflexed murder which is Freud's inverted homicide. It may be reunion, rebirth, self-punishment, or even giving into what one considers a state of already being dead.[43]

Some important clues to the psychodynamics of suicide have been gained in a study of suicide notes. Shneidman and Farberow have made distinctive contributions at this point by study of hundreds of such notes at the Los Angeles Suicide Prevention Center.[44] Analysis of the notes written by those who actually committed suicide as compared to a control group's "make believe" notes, gives a clear view of the thought processes in suicide. The suicidal person thinks and writes in very concrete terms—there's no maybe or perhaps. Reference is very often made to a female person. And there's a strange projection of self beyond death as though one were coming back to check on items discussed. The notes seem to reflect a shift in motivation with increased age from wish to kill to wish to be killed and finally at old age simply the wish to die.

Causes, Dynamics and Motivations

Shneidman, in other research, discusses suicide as representing metaphenomena.[45] This is described as a panic reaction when one realizes that he is becoming disturbed over an upsetting situation. It's a panic at the panic rather than at the source of trouble itself.

Practically all suicidal behavior, says Shneidman, stems from a sense of isolation and from feelings of some intolerable emotion on the part of the victim.[46] The isolation is explained by Hand and Meisel who say, "There is a generalized inability to develop relationships or retain them and a constant negation of relationships or involvement with others despite a seeking for them."[47] One often hears it said of the suicide victim, "He was a loner."

This isolation factor becomes all the more significant when compared with the findings of Tabachnick who points to frequency of intense dependent relationships on the part of suicidal patients.[48] He says these dependent relationships have been threatened prior to many suicidal attempts. An interesting confirmation of this view can be found in Hendin's study of suicide in Denmark. That country's high rate is to be attributed, he says, to a lifelong built-in dependency pattern in Danish culture.[49]

Other cultural patterns such as social isolation, mobility, divorce, and illegitimacy are also significant factors in suicide occurrence.[50] General social norms are important influences as well. Life had to be dangerous and lived near the abyss for Nordic heroes, thus Germany is a classic country of suicide.[51] In Japan, suicide has been used to turn defeat into victory.[52] And the drive for success in Sweden has caused many, fearing failure, to resort to suicide.[53]

In America, suicide problems come in mixed forms. Men more often turn to suicide over concern for physical matters—both bodily and financially, while women despair emotionally over broken relationships. The records of a typical Suicide Prevention Center lists these precipitating causes in their approximate order of frequency:

> Marital problems; alcohol intoxication; love problems; physical illness; loneliness and isolation; problems with children; problems with parents; post-partum depression; failure in school; no relief with private physician.[54]

A study of suicidal patients taking the Minnesota Multiphasic Personality Inventory indicates as common responses depression, frustration, anger, and psychasthenia (anxiety, doubt, inadequacy, and unreality).[55] Those administering the inventory felt, interestingly enough, that a suicidal threat once carried out could actually bring reduction of depression and aggressive feelings. This is an important finding, for while all depression does not lead to suicide and all suicide patients are not necessarily depressed, still depression is probably the most common factor in suicide. With both aggression and depression reduced, the suicide risk is lessened considerably.

Another aspect of suicidal behavior which will have much bearing on discussion of suicide in the armed forces, is the manipulative suicide described by Sifneos.[56] While some using this form succeed in killing themselves, Sifneos describes it as an effort to rearrange the environment in order to go on living.

Before turning from general causes, dynamics, and motivations, two factors are significant to note. Suicide, first of all, is rarely considered to be a baseless impulse, but rather a lengthy process built upon dynamics long at work. And secondly, improvement does not mean the suicide risk is over. Research shows that many actually commit suicide within ninety days of a recovery date.[57] Concern over the dynamics at work in suicide needs to remain constant.

The findings pertaining to causes, dynamics, and motivations among young people, like the general population, indicate first of all a multiple causation. Suicide and suicide attempts are felt to be due to unresolved conflicts, frustration, disappointments, guilt feelings, loss of self-esteem, fear of punishment, and the real or imaginary loss of a love object.[58] Aggression is seen as a strong motivating force at work in youthful suicides, usually directed toward the love object in a punishing way.

Of the various forms of causation, Peck selects loss or separation from a loved one as the major factor.[59] He feels it may assume many forms such as homesickness or awareness of unsatisfied dependency needs.

In a coast to coast survey among helping professionals, a related answer was provided to the question, "What makes teenagers kill themselves?" Though a variety of answers was offered,

Causes, Dynamics and Motivations

the most common was—"the breakdown, or complete lack of communication between parent and adolescent."[60] The impact of this answer appears to be registered for many years into young adulthood.

Dr. Faigel lists four types of suicide among young persons, which he calls "communication suicide."[61] The first is by those who want to live, but they need reassurance that others want them to live too. The second is simply impulsive suicide which involves both suffering and attention, but may accidentally bring death. Thirdly, he describes the balance between a life and death type of suicide, with various clues given to possible death. Finally, there is the want-to-die type when little warning is given.

In another instance, youthful suicide is depicted as not being the attention-seeking, manipulating device, but rather the efforts of an unhappy, helpless, hopeless youngster who desperately wants to change something in his life and is apparently unable to do so in any other way.[62]

Two studies dealing with broken homes and parental deprivation provide possible insight into suicide at this age level. The first study indicates that from a group of seventy patients who had attempted suicide and experienced parental deprivation, the deprivation occured in the first five years of life, which differed significantly from a similar group of nonsuicidal patients.[63] The second study, likewise set up with a suicide and control group, showed that the chief distinction between the two was that the control group had experienced a stable home during the last five years, while the suicide attempts had not.[64] The loss of love is seen, through these two studies, to be significant at either early or late periods. And it is emphasized that the love object may even be lost while still physically present.

David Lester has conducted some interesting research on the relationship of sibling position to suicidal behavior. His data leads him to conclude that it is the oldest and perhaps also youngest children who are over-represented in a group of adolescent suicidal attempts.[65] Apparently greater suppression of outward-directed aggression and over dependency are key factors.

"A pioneer in suicidal prevention," could be the title given Chad Varah of England, who, in addition to his monumental work with the "Samaritans," has focused on problems of young people as well. In a study of sexual and religious conflicts, he concludes: "suicidal young people are almost always troubled about problems arising from their sexual and emotional needs, and the inner conflicts which these create because of their religious or conscientious ideals."[66] So young people experience powerful urges and needs in a society of contrary pressures, and they need loved ones who understand and communicate with them if sorrow and disaster are to be averted.

The special area of college student suicides is of great concern because of the especially high occurrence factor in this group. What is the special pressure or problem for this segment of our society? Answers are mixed and sometimes even contradictory, but there are important findings for our examination.

The most immediate difficulty one would imagine facing college students would be the stress of academic achievement. Yet, it is here that contradictory evidence comes to the fore. For evidence indicates students who committed suicide were those of greater intellectual competence. In one study, students who committed suicide had higher gradepoint averages (3.18 as opposed to 2.50), and a greater number of them had won scholastic awards (58 per cent as opposed to 5 per cent).[67] Generally, suicidal students appear to be doing very well in their academic pursuits.

Yet the presenting complaint of suicidal men students, according to one study, has most often been connected with academic work.[68] Apparently, the difference is to be attributed to how students see their own level of achievement. Frequently the A or B student has been found to feel he is still not doing his best or that he may slip and lose it all. This same study, conducted at Harvard and Radcliffe, showed most men students from Harvard attempting suicide in the freshman year and the lowest number doing so in the senior year, while most women of Radcliffe who attempted suicide did so in the sophomore and senior years and the fewest number attempted during the freshman year. This is explained by the fact that men complained most about academic work, while women were concerned over male-female separations.

Who is the typical college suicide patient? The typical pattern, described by Peck and Schrut is:

a sensitive, lonely, unhappy boy, who may have many acquaintances and even some successes, but who seems to have lacked a close, meaningful relationship. Perhaps the most frequent single comment made about this group of suicides is "No one *really* seemed to know him."[69]

Satisfying interpersonal relationships, beginning with a close family life, seem to be crucial. Dr. Peck would say drugs have been highly overrated as a cause of college suicides, while family relationships, loneliness, and disappointment in love have been vastly underrated.[70]

Depression seems to continue in college students as in other suicide patients, but in a different form. It is not so much a feeling of painful dejection, loss of interest, or inhibition of activity, but rather a feeling of fluctuation in self-esteem.[71] Healthy self-esteem for the college student means developing a healthy body image, achieving harmony between the self-concept and the ego ideal, and creating a capacity for love, tenderness, and intimacy.

And finally, students can become seriously depressed over the gap between their idealism and society's materialism. They become angry and finally depressed with institutionalization and depersonalization.[72] Sometimes they can externalize this anger with violence or repress it with alcohol, but for many it becomes internalized and fatal.

Our fifth and final research area, and the focus of our attention, is the young adult in the armed forces. In some ways he is similar to other young people in his suicidal reactions; and in many other respects his is quite different.

He is similar in his feelings of aloneness and loneliness. Like many a suicidal college youth, the military youth is usually typified as "the man nobody knows." In one study of forty-two suicidal patients six noted that they had good friends or got along well with their peers, either past or present.[73]

Military young adults, likewise, feel a strong need to resolve their conflicts with an intense urgency, but how they go about doing so is different from other suicidals, perhaps because the young military man is in a way so different himself. There is also the difference of the problems he confronts.

Unlike the college youth, the military suicidal patient is not generally doing well in his world of work. He has been unsuccessful in completing his education and, in military life, he has failed to rise above the lowest levels. Figures compiled, for special use in this crisis study, at San Diego and Oakland Naval Hospitals for 1964-65 indicate a high percentage of the suicidal patients did not complete high school.[74] Table 11 shows the listings by grades. San Diego's less than eighth grade figure represents only one man in that category. There were 152 males and 6 females studied at San Diego, with 227 males and 6 females at Oakland.

TABLE 11

Percentages of Total Psychiatric Patient Population with Suicidal Tendencies: 1964-65*

Education	San Diego	Oakland
Less than 8th grade	100.0	14.3
8th grade	40.0	21.4
9th grade	36.4	28.1
10th grade	40.0	25.1
11th grade	41.7	27.8
12th grade	37.7	30.0
13th grade	33.3	0.0

* From Navy Medical Neuropsychiatric Research Unit, San Diego, California, December 12, 1969. (Typewritten.)

Suicidal tendencies were also found to be much higher in the patients of lower pay grades. Figures between 36.2 per cent and 43.4 per cent were typical for the number of low pay grade patients showing suicidal tendencies. While in higher pay grades percentages of suicidal tendencies generally ran between 16.7 and 33.3 per cent.[75]

Fisch discovered that out of a group of 114 suicide patients only 23 were above the grade of seaman in the Navy or private first class in the Marine Corps.[76]

Hauschild, among others, picks up a striking fact in the diagnosis of young military suicides. Unlike other groups, he discovers only about 19 per cent of the 1471 suicidal patients

Causes, Dynamics and Motivations

studied over a ten-year period suffered from depression. Rather, 52.34 per cent were classified as character and behavior disorders—generally described as emotionally immature and unstable.[77] San Diego Naval Hospital reported two-thirds of their suicidal patients as character and behavior disorders.[78] Depression was a factor for 43 patients, while it was not for 115. In Oakland, depression was a factor for 42 and was not for 191. Newby and Van Der Heide found the character and behavior disorder diagnosis running 68 per cent in their study of 139 patients.[79] This variation from the typical dynamic pattern is seen as less turning of aggression inward, but instead using it to mold external environment, which sets up the central characteristic of military young adult suicide.

Tucker, Reinhardt, Offenkrantz, Church, Elliott, and virtually all others studying this area concur in classifying young adult military suicidal behavior as primarily manipulative. Tucker and Reinhardt say that 73 per cent of the forty-two military patients they worked with stated directly at admission, "Let me out of the service."[80] And the striking fact, which Tucker and Reinhardt show along with others, is that these young men are amazingly successful in achieving their goal—probably, as one researcher indicates, for one of the few times in their lives. Among Tucker and Reinhardt's patients, 67 per cent were released from the service; suprisingly enough, 48 per cent achieved this without psychiatric help but through other avenues, after being released from the Psychiatric Service. Compare this with Tucker and Reinhardt's control group of general psychiatric patients in which only 35 per cent were discharged and only 8 per cent accomplished it later without psychiatric aid. This is a testimony to the urgency of suicidal patients and their manipulative ability.

It might be well to note, as Newby and Van Der Heide suggest, that such heightened manipulation in the form of suicidal gesture may be related to the rigidities, regimentation, and hierarchy of authority within the military system which makes it difficult for the individual to alter unsatisfactory conditions.[81]

Tucker and Reinhardt could find no particular difference in suicidal family histories as compared to other patients; Hauschild did indicate that father loss was three times mother loss.[82] Repeat suicide attempts were found to be common and these patients not only evidenced poor peer relations, but showed more impulsive behavior and poor authority relations. They were poor achievers in further military service as well as upon return to civilian life.[83]

One study emphasizes the diagnosis of "immaturity reactions," saying that suicidal acts are most often performed by the youngest of the military young adults.[84] "Insecure," "inadequate," and "immature personalities," are descriptions used in most studies along with the general category of character and behavior disorder.

Pozner brings understanding to the female suicide in the military, saying that women commit suicide for emotional and subjective reasons, while men appear more concerned with principles and objective causes.[85] Women are said to fear loneliness, loss of love objects, humiliation, and responsibilities.

In general, alcohol and drugs do not appear to be particularly significant in military suicidal behavior.[86] This holds true back to the World War II study in which no more than eleven per cent showed alcohol present to the extent of affecting judgement.[87] That study concluded there was a three to one probability suicide was the cause of death in unnatural occurrences with negative alcohol findings. Apparently the suicidal does not need the narcotic bolstering and is fully conscious of his actions. This seems to be true with the use of drugs as well. The San Diego Naval Hospital study shows 127 patients did not use drugs as compared to 31 who did. The Oakland Hospital figures indicate 182 did not and 51 did.[88]

From an Air Force study by Eggertsen, evidence is presented that suicide rates are lower overseas because of escape from home pressures, and because of ties within the "island of American culture." There is also suggestion offered that the particular military group or command one is with might affect suicide rates. The Air Force Continental Air Command, for 1958-1964, showed rates of 21.8 per 100,000, while the lowest rates for the same period were in the USAF Security Service with 5.3 per 100,000.[89] Additional research in this area could be helpful.

A look at suicidal patients during the Viet Nam crisis reveals some interesting facets of suicidal activity among young adults in the armed forces.

A study conducted aboard the hospital ship *Repose* revealed a relatively infrequent occurrence of suicidal attempts and threats among the psychiatric patient population—eight per cent.[90] This is compared with a Navy hospital psychiatric population in the continental United States where such suicidal activity was noted in twenty-four per cent of the patients. The infrequent occurrence in a combat area tends to support the common theory that suicide activity is reduced in times of war and in combat areas. The externalization of aggression in combat apparently serves to decrease the self-directed violence.

However, as doctors Strange and Brown would remind us, one may perceive a particular expression of aggressive talk and threats of self-destruction among Viet Nam returnees. They are quick to indicate the talk and threats do not appear to be followed by action.[91] While twenty-six per cent of the patients in their study exhibited suicidal threats or preoccupations, only sixteen per cent actually carried out attempts or gestures. Yet it might be noted that this acting out percentage for returnees is double the percentage of combat personnel aboard the hospital ship. Might one not raise a question about preoccupations and threats eventually leading to destructive behavior on the part of a certain percentage of returnee patients?

Such behavior among Viet Nam returnees could well be explained by the findings of two physicians contained in an article dramatically titled, "Unhappy Odysseys." Goldsmith and Cretekos indicate how the Viet Nam returnees frequently asked, "What was I doing there?"[92] The question seemed to not only reflect confusion about the war, but possibly the magical expectation that one's life situation would somehow be better when he returns. The returnee often thinks, "I've gone through the ritual—where is the happy ending?" The post-combat period appears for many to contain continued disillusionment described by some as feelings of being "boxed in." Patients with these feelings have often developed a fatalistic attitude, turned to indifference, and finally deterioration leading to possibly a form of self-destruction.

Dr. Langner describes a Navy corpsman named Bob who represents a certain response of some who've encountered the full horrors of Viet Nam. Bob was himself involved in an incident like the My Lai massacre.[93] Before it was over, this corpsman had, at his own admission, "set fields of rice ablaze," watched "peasants shot down as they ran from their burning homes," and finally himself "shot and killed" an elderly injured farmer lying at his feet. Bob experienced deep guilt after this and felt he should be punished for his crime. When his friend, a fellow corpsman, was killed several weeks later, Bob wished he could have died in his place. This thus served as the precipitant for Bob's suicide attempt.

Some of the experiences from Viet Nam which are virtually unprecedented in American history have also provided us with some self-destructive dynamics unique to that situation.

Two follow-up factors should be remembered. Once identified as "suicidal," psychiatric patients have suicide rates four times that of psychiatric patients generally. And of all known subsequent successful suicides, 84.4 per cent had occurred within one year of discharge.[94]

NOTES

1. Shneidman and Farberow, eds., *Clues to Suicide*, p. 11.
2. *Ibid.*
3. *Ibid.*
4. Arthur L. Kobler and Ezra Stotland, *The End of Hope* (New York: The Macmillan Company, 1964), p. 4.
5. Shneidman and Mandelkorn, *How To Prevent Suicide*, p. 8.
6. Prediction and Prevention of Suicide," *Canada Medical Association Journal*, C (May 10, 1969), p. 867.
7. Shneidman and Mandelkorn, *How To Prevent Suicide*, p. 8.
8. "Prediction and and Prevention of Suicide," p. 867.
9. Pokorny, "Suicide, Suicide Attempts, and Weather," p. 381.
10. Sigmund Freud, "Mourning and Melancholia," *Collected Papers*, IV (London: Hogarth Press, Ltd., 1948), p. 162.
11. *Ibid.*
12. Farberow and Shneidman, *The Cry For Help*, p. 169.
13. G. Bollea and R. Mayer, "Psychopathology of Suicide in the Formative Years," *Acta Paedopsychiat (Basel)*, XXXV (December, 1968), p. 338.
14. Menninger, *Man Against Himself*, p. 82.
15. *Ibid.*, p. 35.
16. Castelli, "Suicide—The Whispered Word," p. 9.
17. Otto Fenichel, *The Psychoanalytic Theory of Neurosis* (New York: W. W. Norton and Company, Inc., 1945), p. 294.
18. *Ibid.*, p. 401.
19. James A. Knight, *A Psychiatrist Looks at Religion and Health* (New York: Abingdon Press, 1964), p. 102.

20. Beall, "The Dynamics of Suicide: A Review of the Literature, 1897-1965," p. 3.
21. Durkheim, *Suicide*, p. 169.
22. *Ibid.*, p. 221.
23. *Ibid.*, p. 234.
24. *Ibid.*, p. 246.
25. *Ibid.*, p. 63.
26. Shneidman and Farberow, eds., *Clues to Suicide*, p. 14.
27. *Ibid.*
28. Beall, "The Dynamics of Suicide: A Review of the Literature, 1897-1965," p. 4.
29. C. G. Jung, "The Soul and Death," translated by R. P. C. Hull, in H. Feifel, ed., *The Meaning of Death* (New York: McGraw-Hill Book Company, Inc., 1959), p. 6.
30. Farberow and Shneidman, *The Cry For Help*, p. 204.
31. *Ibid.*, p. 220.
32. *Ibid.*, p. 236.
33. Victor E. Frankl, *Man's Search For Meaning* (New York: Washington Square Press, Inc., 1963), p. xi.
34. Dublin, *Factbook on Man From Birth to Death*, p. 258.
35. Stengel, *Suicide and Attempted Suicide*, p. 69.
36. Farberow and Shneidman, *The Cry for Help*, pp. 19-46.
37. James Hillman, *Suicide and the Soul* (New York: Harper and Row, Publishers, 1964), p. 63.
38. Farberow and Shneidman, *The Cry for Help*, p. 297.
39. R. E. Litman, T. Curphey, and E. Shneidman, "Investigations of Equivocal Suicides," *Journal of the American Medical Association*, CLXXXIV (1963), p. 927.
40. Yolles, *The Tragedy of Suicide in the U.S.*, p. 3.
41. Berblinger, "Suicide as a Message," p. 145.
42. *Ibid.*, p. 146.
43. Herbert Hendin, *Suicide and Scandinavia* (New York: Grune and Stratton, Inc., 1964), pp. 19-25.
44. Feifel, ed., *The Meaning of Death*, pp. 292-295.
45. Edwin S. Shneidman, "Suicide, Sleep and Death," *Journal of Consulting Psychology*, XXVIII, No. 2 (1964), p. 2.
46. Edwin S. Shneidman, "Preventing Suicide," *The American Journal of Nursing*, LXV, No. 5 (May, 1965), p. 2.
47. Morton H. Hand and Arthur M. Meisel, "Dynamic Aspects of Suicide," *New York State Journal of Medicine*, LXVI (December 1, 1966), p. 3009.
48. Leston L. Havens, "Diagnosis of Suicidal Intent," *Annual Review of Medicine*, XX (1969), p. 422.
49. Hendin, *Suicide and Scandinavia*, pp. 30-35.
50. J. W. McCulloch, A. E. Philip and G. M. Carstairs, "The Ecology

of Suicidal Behavior," *British Journal of Psychiatry,* CXIII (March, 1967), p. 313.

51. Meerloo, *Suicide and Mass Suicide,* p. 75.
52. Knight, *A Psychiatrist Looks At Religion and Health,* p. 109.
53. Hendin, *Suicide and Scandinavia,* p. 45.
54. H. H. Brunt Jr., M. Rotor, and T. Glenn, "A Suicide Prevention Center in a Public Mental Hospital," *Mental Hygiene,* LII (April, 1968), p. 258.
55. W. G. Dahstrom and C. S. Welsh, *An MMPI Handbook* (Minneapolis: The University of Minnesota Press, 1960), p. 321.
56. Peter E. Sifneos, "Manipulative Suicide," *Psychiatric Quarterly,* XL (July, 1966), p. 529.
57. Knight, *A Psychiatrist Looks At Religion and Health,* pp. 120-121.
58. Edwin S. Shneidman, "Suicide Among Adolescents," *California School Health* (October, 1966), p. 2.
59. Michael L. Peck, "Suicide Motivations in Adolescents," *Adolescence,* III, No. 9 (Spring, 1968), p. 113.
60. "The Better Way," *Good Housekeeping* (October, 1969), p. 208.
61. Faigel, "Suicide Among Young Persons," p. 188.
62. Peck, "Suicide Motivations in Adolescents," p. 188.
63. N. McConaghy, J. Linane, and R. C. Buckle, "Parental Deprivation and Attempted Suicide," *The Medical Journal of Australia,* I (May 21, 1966), p. 892.
64. J. Jacobs and J. D. Teicher, "Broken Homes and Social Isolation in Attempted Suicides of Adolescents," *International Journal of Social Psychiatry,* XIII (Spring, 1967), p. 146.
65. David Lester, "Sibling Position and Suicidal Behavior," *Journal of Individual Psychology,* XXII (November, 1966), p. 206.
66. Chad Varah, "Sexual and Religious Conflicts in Suicidal Young People," *Zeitschrift für Präventivmedizin,* X (1965), p. 487.
67. Richard H. Seiden, "Studies of Adolescent Suicidal Behavior," *Suicide Among Youth* (Chevy Chase, Maryland: NIMH, December, 1969), p. 38.
68. Graham B. Blaine Jr. and Lida R. Carmen, "Brief Communications: Causal Factors in Suicidal Attempts by Male and Female College Students," *American Journal of Psychiatry,* CXXV (December 6, 1968), p. 835.
69. Michael L. Peck and Albert Schrut, "Suicide Among College Students," Paper presented at Fourth International Conference for Suicide Prevention at Los Angeles, October 19, 1967, p. 7. (Mimeographed.)
70. *Ibid.,* p. 1.
71. Preston K. Munter, "Depression and Suicide in College Students," Paper of Harvard University Health Services, p. 20. (Mimeographed.)
72. *Ibid.,* p. 23.
73. Tucker and Gorman, "The Significance of the Suicide Gesture in the Military," p. 859.

Causes, Dynamics and Motivations

74. Navy Medical Neuropsychiatric Research Unit, "Percentages of Patient Groups with Suicidal Tendencies," San Diego, California, December 12, 1969. (Typewritten.)

75. *Ibid.*

76. Mayer Fisch, "The Suicidal Gesture: A Study of 114 Military Patients Hospitalized Because of Abortive Suicide Attempts," *American Journal of Psychiatry,* III (1954), p. 33.

77. Thomas B. Hauschild, "Suicidal Population of a Military Psychiatric Center: A Review of Ten Years," *Military Medicine,* CXXXIII (June, 1968), p. 427.

78. Navy Medical Neuropsychiatric Research Unit, "Percentages of Patient Groups with Suicidal Tendencies," San Diego, California, December 12, 1969. (Typewritten.)

79. John H. Newby Jr. and C. J. Van Der Heide, "A Review of 139 Suicidal Gestures: Discussion of Some Psychological Implications and Treatment Techniques," *Military Medicine,* CXXXIII (August, 1968), p. 630.

80. Tucker and Reinhardt, "Suicide Attempts," p. 17.

81. Newby and Van Der Heide, "A Review of 139 Suicidal Gestures," p. 629.

82. Hauschild, "Suicidal Population of a Military Psychiatric Center," p. 433.

83. Tucker and Reinhardt, "Suicide Attempts," p. 17.

84. Offenkrantz, Church, and Elliott, "Psychiatric Management of Suicide Problems in Military Service," p. 37.

85. Pozner, "Suicidal Incidents in Military Personnel," p. 101.

86. Hauschild, "Suicidal Population of a Military Psychiatric Center," p. 429.

87. Zamcheck and Geisler, "Homicides and Suicides of World War II," p. 91.

88. Navy Medical Neuropsychiatric Research Unit, "Percentages of Patient Groups with Suicidal Tendencies," San Diego, California, December 12, 1969. (Typewritten.)

89. Eggertsen, "Suicide by Air Force Personnel 1958 to 1964," pp. 28-30.

90. Robert E. Strange and Ransom J. Arthur, "Hospital Ship Psychiatry in a War Zone," *The American Journal of Psychiatry,* CXXIV, No. 3 (1967), p. 281.

91. Robert E. Strange and Dudley E. Brown, "Home From the War: A Study of Psychiatric Problems in Viet Nam Returnees," *The American Journal of Psychiatry,* CXXVII, No. 4 (1970), p. 488.

92. William Goldsmith and Constantine Cretekos, "Unhappy Odysseys," *Archives of General Psychiatry,* XX (Jan. 1969), p. 78.

93. Herman P. Langner, "The Making of a Murderer," *The American Journal of Psychiatry,* CXXVII, No. 7 (1971), p. 126.

94. Hauschild, "Suicidal Population of a Military Psychiatric Center," p. 435.

4. Symptoms and Characteristics

VERBAL CLUES

Hauschild tells of a Private First Class who while awaiting administrative discharge for homosexuality, jumped to his death.[1] He was found to have been immature and impulsive, but not mentally ill or depressed. A CID investigation did bring out that he had made suicidal threats to friends on some four occasions when he had been drinking.

Experts in Suicidology tell us that "of any ten people who kill themselves, eight have given definite warning."[2] One of the most common myths about suicide which should be quickly dispelled is that those who talk about suicide don't carry it out. Evidence shows they are the very ones who do commit suicide. In over half the suicide deaths, there is a history of spontaneous suicidal communications giving clues to those who could or would perceive them. These precursors to suicide called "prodromal clues" are vital keys to helping the suicidal. As a number of authorities indicate, the real cause of suicide, in final analysis, may be the failure of someone to respond when help is sought. The prodromal clue is in essence the cry for help, and the most obvious of those clues is the verbal statement.

The following are examples of statements people have actually made who later killed themselves:

> "My family would be better off without me." "I'm going to end it all; I can't stand this any more." "I won't be around much longer for you to put up with me." "I don't want to be a burden." "This is the last straw; this is all I needed." "I can't stand it any longer. I want to die."[3]

Some verbal clues are quite direct as most of the above, while others are considered indirect such as:

Symptoms and Characteristics

"It's too much to put up with." "Farewell." "How do you leave your body to the medical school?" "I won't need this club card any longer." "How do you shoot this gun?" "Could the family get along without me?"[4]

Many verbal clues are given in coded verbal communication which is more subtle and may require "decoding." Messages may be spoken like these:

"This is the last time I'll ever be here." "This is the last shot you'll ever give me." "Goodbye, Miss Jones, I won't be here when you come back." "What could be done to help a friend of mine who's thinking of suicide?"[5]

Before giving straight answers or responses to many of the above illustrations, one would do well to inquire further about the meaning. Whose body is being given to the medical school? What friend is considering suicide?

While a majority of people making statements similar to these verbal clues do not go on to commit suicide, authorities warn that it is dangerous to take any such statements lightly. Most fatal suicide acts are preceded by similar remarks.

Sometimes these remarks are made to a physician or professional counselor; but they are more often made before friends and relatives. Most suicide cases show a long history of such signals that went completely unnoticed. It is essential to understand and respond helpfully to these verbal clues.

PHYSICAL SIGNS

Research indicates that three-fourths of all who commit suicide have seen a physician within at least four months of the day on which they take their lives.[6] Thus, the very factor of recent physical or mental illness becomes important to perception of suicide symptoms. It is vital to recognize, further, the nature of the physical problems for which medical assistance is sought.

When people are suicidal they are generally disturbed. The one overriding symptom is a manifestation of feelings of depression.[7] They feel hopeless about the direction of their lives and helpless to do anything about it. There is often a sinking into increased pessimism until only death is left.

The sleeping pattern is an interesting aspect of suicidal symptoms. On one hand, insomnia may plague the patient with interruptions of sleep, coming especially in the early morning hours. But in contrast, which perhaps develops as the patient moves closer to serious action, sleep may become increasingly longer and deeper. At this point, Shneidman says, "both sleep and suicide can be seen as metaphenomena, i.e., as secondary reactions to more substantive occurrences."[8] Sleep apparently becomes an escape from the world before the final sleep. Waking up has brought reported feelings of "miserable," "discouraged," and "having no hope." Nightmares and dreams of running off for protection may occur.

The suicidal individual is likely to be morose and isolated more than usual. He is inclined to worry more and suffer loss of appetite. This is accompanied by feelings of "being beaten," wanting to hide and of having no rewarding experiences.[9]

One needs to realize, however, that such deep feelings may lie far below surface appearances and even be in contrast to them. Some potential suicides may mask their disturbance with a gay and frivolous manner while speaking of past accomplishments and triumphs.

Dr. Jacobziner says warning signs in children are "a sudden and persistent change in personality or behavior, agitation, anxiety, irritability, depression, anorexia, insomnia, and frequent and unnecessary outbursts of temper."[10]

In addition to "pushing himself too hard" and being worried about grades not being as good as they should be, the college student is likely to worry about body deterioration. Failing eyes, stomachache, and drastic weight loss are concerns which do in fact materialize into realities and precipitate suicidal behavior.[11]

Specific military personnel indicators of suicidal tendencies are reported to include: complaints of nervousness, sleeping and adjustment difficulties, feelings of discomfort, longing for home, and expressions of a condition of insufficiency.[12]

The person of suicidal tendencies may indeed have physical or emotional problems, but it is essential to recognize the greater problem of life itself to which they point.

Symptoms and Characteristics

PERSONAL ACTIONS

Certain characteristics of behavior are indicative of the suicidal and serve as significant clues to sensitive observers. Attention should be especially given to steps of termination such as giving away prized possessions, like a watch, earrings, golf clubs, or heirlooms. Making a will, putting affairs in order, or taking a lengthy trip under peculiar circumstances should be looked upon as possible signals for help.[13]

Researchers in semantics, logic, and thought expression are providing important new insights into peculiarities of reasoning in the suicidal.[14] Suicide notes apparently point this up clearly as anything immediately at hand. Temporarily, at least, the suicide patient seems to set aside normal inductive or deductive logic so that conclusions just do not follow logically. His spurious logic, which tends toward singular and negative answers, can actually be decisive in tripping the suicide patient over life's edge.

Young males seem to find particular difficulty in openly expressing emotional feelings and problems. The young man of suicidal tendency may quietly allow turmoil to brew inside, while to others he appears to be the "quiet," "normal," "good" boy. The only behavior he may display as a clue to suicide could well be spiritless obedience and withdrawal.[15] This behavior may be interpreted by some as terribly shy, asocial, or unfriendliness.

This type of behavior among college students might be reflected in increased study to the point of total absorption in schoolwork. A most calamitous example of this human isolation was the case of a student, dead for eighteen days before he was found in his lonely room.[16] This was not only a tragic commentary on his existence, but the lack of someone who would care enough to find out about his death in less than two and a half weeks, was probably also a cause of his suicide.

While the withdrawn behavior may be most characteristic of suicides, it is necessary to also understand how the opposite behavior may be evidenced.[17] People involved in stormy love affairs, for example, may be seen in an outpouring of rejected feelings of anguish. Such critical feelings from a complete disruption of personal relationships may be the last straw for one already perilously close to the edge.

Any radical change in behavior, particularly if accompanied by psychological difficulty, disheveled appearance, weight loss, worried or depressed attitude, should be considered as possibly symptomatic of suicide tendency. The concern would be justifiably increased if the person also demonstrates an inability to get work done. Freud's gauges for mental health—to be able to love and to work—are also key indicators of one's possible suicide potential.

The clues to possible suicide are thus readily available to almost any sensitive person who cares enough to see and respond to one whose life is hanging in the balance. While some authorities feel that more clues are likely given by younger rather than older persons, and by the attempts more often than those determined to die, the consensus is still that in virtually all, the desire for life is as strong as any impulse to die. Hearing, seeing, and responding with helpful concern can make all the difference.

NOTES

1. Hauschild, "Suicide in Europe," p. 251.
2. Whiteley, "Student Stress, Suicide, and the Role of the University," p. 121.
3. *Ibid.*, p. 122.
4. Hauschild, "Suicide in Europe," p. 251.
5. Shneidman, "Preventing Suicide," p. 3.
6. Shneidman and Mandelkorn, *How to Prevent Suicide*, p. 12.
7. *Ibid.*
8. Shneidman, "Suicide, Sleep and Death," p. 103.
9. Hand and Meisel, "Dynamic Aspects of Suicide," p. 3009.
10. Shneidman, "Suicide Among Adolescents," p. 2.
11. Richard H. Seiden, "Campus Tragedy: A Study of Student Suicide," *Journal of Abnormal Psychology*, LXX (December, 1966), p. 397.
12. Otto, "Suicidal Attempts Made During Compulsory Military Service," p. 306.
13. Shneidman, "Preventing Suicide," p. 3.
14. Shneidman and Mandelkorn, *How to Prevent Suicide*, p. 19.
15. Peck, "Suicide Motivations in Adolescents," p. 112.
16. Seiden, "Campus Tragedy: A Study of Student Suicide," p. 398.
17. *Ibid.*

5. Methods of Suicide

BOTH SEXES

Several matters of crucial significance are related to the method employed in a suicidal act. The choice of technique one makes for self-destruction will, first of all, probably determine the success or failure of the act. This in itself makes the method employed an additional clue to the "lethality" of an attempt.[1] The more violent means such as shooting, hanging, jumping, or stabbing are far more lethal than pills or poisons; and they generally communicate a message of fatal intent. Methods of a less lethal nature are more often interpreted as a desperate and dramatic call for attention and assistance. Studies are also being conducted to determine whether the choice of method is in any way related to the personality of the victim. If conclusive evidence should be forthcoming, this might well serve as an additional aid in recognizing potential problems.

Stengel, among others, has dealt with the availability factor in methods of suicide. He concludes that the availability of a particular method does not in itself determine choice of that method.[2] Some figures may cause questioning of this, however, especially among medical people and military personnel in general. Stengel also feels that a shift from one method to another often appears in large cross sections of the population, but with such change there is little or no reduction in suicide occurrence.[3]

Perhaps the violence of our society is reflected in the methods chosen for suicide. Dublin tells us that 90 per cent of those who die by their own hand use one of three methods—shooting, hanging, or poisoning.[4] While the more violent means have been customarily attributed to men, it is notable that women are reported to be increasingly choosing more violent methods.

Geography and culture seem to also have a bearing on the

technique selected for suicide. Ancient and oriental cultures are often described as more imaginative and diversified in their procedures for self-destruction. Japan today, in contrast to the West, is reported to employ soporific drugs in 90 per cent of its completed suicides.[5] Differences have been pointed out between the east and west coast methods in the United States. Table 12 shows the different order of frequent selection between the United States as a whole and New York City.

TABLE 12

Comparison of Popular Methods of Suicide
1966*-1971†

United States Suicides*	New York City Suicides†
Most Frequent	
1. Firearms and explosives	Poisons
2. Poisons or gases	Gases
3. Hanging	Jumping from high places
4. Drowning	Hanging
5. Jumping from high places	Firearms
6. Cutting or piercing instruments	Cutting or piercing instruments
Least Frequent	
7. Other	Other

*Small and De Armond, "The Clinical Assessment and Management of the Potential Suicide," p. 1303.
†"Most City Suicides Called Preventable," *New York Times* (Sept. 26, 1971), p. 60.

The most dramatic differences, as implied in these chapter divisions, are to be found between the methods selected by men as compared to women's selections. In this first section we shall continue looking at common factors in the selections of both sexes, then turn to an examination of each individually.

When suicide methods are observed to be cruel, ghastly self-mutilations, these are most often inferred to be the result of twisted minds suffering from depression or schizophrenia.[6] In such cases, the suicide may follow other homicidal acts.

Physician deaths from suicide reported in the *American*

Medical Association Journal for May, 1966, gave some surprising information regarding one method employed. An investigation team presented what they called an "alarming statistic" for deaths by aircraft accidents. The annual death rate for physicians with respect to private aircraft is approximately nine times that for white males who die in private aircraft accidents.[7]

The automobile accident offers another method of suicide widely employed and most difficult to document. Yet one study has produced figures which indicate that thirty-three suicidal people had 2.70 accidents per person compared to a matched control group record of 1.30 per person for the same period of time.[8] Another study by Faigel reports that ten patients out of thirty who attempted to drive to their deaths struck other vehicles with their own.[9] Thus, suicide by automobile becomes a life or death matter for many people besides the suicidal.

Among college students, both sexes appear to present quite similar patterns in choice of methods. The attempters, as documented at Harvard and Radcliffe, first of all choose pills. The figures were 60 per cent for the women and 52 per cent for the men. The second choice involved cutting—23 per cent for men and 15 per cent for the women.[10] However, of those students who actually committed suicide, according to a California study, fully 50 per cent died by gunshot.[11] Violence and lethality again are equated.

Obviously, among the categories of chronic, social, or organic suicide, which is slowly carried out against oneself for perhaps years, the methods may embrace an almost unlimited number of self-destructive devices from alcohol or drugs to imagined diseases and even obsessive surgery.

Table 13 gives the per cent for total U.S. male and female choice of methods for suicide and suicide attempt.

MALE

In most sections of society and in most cultures around the world, males tend to use different methods for suicide than do women. In the main, as indicated, male methods are more violent and more likely to result in completed suicide. Whether the methods employed cause completed suicide or whether men

TABLE 13

Methods of Suicide and Suicide Attempt
Both Sexes: United States

Method	Committed suicide Per cent: 1965*	Attempted suicide Per cent: 1957†
Gunshot and explosives	46	3
Hanging	15	1
Barbiturates	13	48
Carbon monoxide, auto	11	1
Poisoning	4	9
Jumping	3	1
Illuminating gas	1	3
Drowning	3	0
Cut throat	2	3
Stabbing	1	1
Cut wrist	1	15
Unknown	3	16

*"World Health Statistics Report," p. 412.
†Farberow and Shneidman, *The Cry for Help*, p. 35.

TABLE 14

Methods of Suicide and Suicide Attempt
Male: United States

Method	Committed suicide Per cent: 1965*	Attempted suicide Per cent: 1957†
Gunshot and explosives	54	5
Hanging	16	2
Carbon monoxide, auto	11	2
Barbiturates	6	34
Poisoning	3	9
Jumping	3	1
Illuminating gas	1	4
Stabbing	1	1
Drowning	2	0
Cut throat	1	6
Cut wrist	1	20
Unknown	2	15

*"World Health Statistics Report," p. 412.
†Farberow and Shneidman, *The Cry for Help*, p. 35.

Methods of Suicide

want to actually commit suicide, and therefore choose the most guaranteed means, is a good question awaiting further research.

Three violent means appear most often among those used by men who commit suicide. The three listed with their per cent of usage among young men aged twenty-twenty-four are: firearms and explosives—59 per cent; poisoning—22 per cent; hanging and strangulation—12 per cent.[12]

Figures from the armed forces can be taken to represent basically a male population. This is perhaps especially true in light of Dr. Eggertsen's finding that women in the service are increasingly choosing firearms over other suicide methods, which he thinks may reflect the man culture in which they live.[13] Neither does Dr. Eggertsen find any significant difference of methods between different races in service life. A typical military listing of methods showing percentage choice of 1179 committed suicides is in Table 15.

TABLE 15

Methods of Committed Suicide: 1941-45*

Method	Per cent
Shooting	49.4
Hanging	23.3
Poisoning	7.8
Stabbing	6.4
Jumping from high place	4.6
Asphyxiation—illuminating gas	2.4
Asphyxiation—motor exhaust	2.1
Jumping from moving vehicle	1.3
Drowning	1.1
Others	1.6

*Zamcheck and Geisler, "Homicides and Suicides of World War II," p. 89.

Another study showing military attempts indicates the striking difference between these and the commit group (Table 16). The most obvious and startling contrast is with shooting, which heads the commit list and hardly appears among attempters. This can be seen to approximate civilian male and total population findings. Males of civilian and military background indicate higher percentages for hangings than the total population. The use of drugs and wrist cutting among both civilian and military men are a strong indication of attempt probabilities rather than actual suicide.

TABLE 16

Methods of Attempted Suicides*
1964-1967

Method	Per cent
Overdose of drugs	57
Laceration	30
Hanging	4
Jumping	4
Drowning	2
Swallowing objects	2
Gas	—
Shooting	—

*Newby and Van Der Heide, "A Review of 139 Suicidal Gestures," p. 633.

FEMALE

Women bring a radically different statistical picture into the study of suicide methods. No total population listing by itself could reveal the characteristic female choice. Their selection is dictated by the rates they show for attempted rather than completed suicide. Again, research has yet to determine how much the method choice of women is influenced by attempt desires, and how much the method determines attempted rather than completed results.

Table 17 shows the choice of methods in per cent as selected by women in the United States who commit or attempt suicide.

A comparison of statistics from previous years in the United States indicates continued high rates for firearms and explosives. Vital statistics from 1955 are virtually identical to 1965 in this category. However, two other areas show radical changes. While hanging and strangulation is still ranked second highest in usage

TABLE 17

Methods of Suicide and Suicide Attempt
Female: United States

Method	Committed suicide Per cent: 1965*	Attempted suicide Per cent: 1957†
Barbiturates	31	54
Gunshot and explosives	24	1
Hanging	12	1
Poisoning	6	9
Carbon monoxide, auto	9	—
Drowning	4	0
Jumping	5	1
Cut throat	2	2
Illuminating gas	1	3
Stabbing	1	1
Cut wrist	0	12
Unknown	5	17

*"World Health Statistics Report," p. 412.
†Farberow and Shneidman, *The Cry for Help*, p. 35.

for the total population, it has decreased 40 to 50 per cent in all group ratings. The decrease in hanging and strangulation has been more than offset by the increase of barbiturates in all groups by more than 50 per cent (Table 18).

TABLE 18

Methods Used for Committing Suicide
Guns, Hanging, Strangulation, and
Barbiturates: United States*

Method	Both Sexes Per cent 1955	1965	Male Per cent 1955	1965	Female Per cent 1955	1965
Guns and explosives	46	47	52	54	25	24
Hanging and strangulation	22	15	20	16	24	12
Barbiturates	6	13	3	6	15	31

*"World Health Statistics Report," p. 412.

One might conclude that the increased traffic in drugs along with continued availability of firearms has had a most dramatic effect upon this nation's choice of methods in suicide.

NOTES

1. Offenkrantz, Church, and Elliott, "Psychiatric Management of Suicide Problems in Military Service," p. 37.
2. Stengel, *Suicide and Attempted Suicide*, p. 33.
3. *Ibid.*, p. 35.
4. Dublin, *Factbook on Man From Birth to Death*, p. 262.
5. Small and De Armond, "The Clinical Assessment and Management of the Potential Suicide," p. 1302.
6. Morhauser, *Suicide*, p. 2.
7. *Ibid.*, p. 13.
8. Melvin L. Selzer and Charles E. Payne, "Automobile Accidents, Suicide and Unconscious Motivations," *American Journal of Psychiatry*, CXIX, No. 3 (1962), p. 237.
9. Faigel, "Suicide Among Young Persons," p. 189.
10. Blaine and Carmen, "Causal Factors in Suicidal Attempts by Male and Female College Students," p. 834.
11. Peck and Schrut, "Suicide Among College Students," p. 4.
12. Seiden, *Suicide Among Youth*, p. 23.
13. Eggertsen, "Suicide by Air Force Personnel 1958 to 1964," p. 29.

6. Clinical Findings

FOCUS, NEEDS, AND DESIGN

The focus of these clinical findings is directed specifically to the problem of actual suicide and attempted suicide among persons seventeen to twenty-five years of age on active duty in the United States Armed Forces. The problem of suicide occurrence has been shown to be particularly high among young adults in general, and almost equally high among the armed forces in particular. In the armed forces, far more may be at stake than the life or welfare of one single individual. However, very little comprehensive study has been directed to understanding and

Clinical Findings

preventing suicides in the armed forces. This clinical research was undertaken with the hope of understanding, more fully, the basic dynamic involved in youthful suicides and attempts among armed forces personnel, and what might be helpful measures for treatment and prevention of suicides. The focus of effective Christian ministry, as one of the concerned disciplines, will be a background consideration to be pursued further in chapters seven and eight.

The need for this research is based primarily on the tragedy of needless loss of life. Other causes of death may rank higher statistically than suicide, but none could be more unnecessarily wasteful of human life. If something is to be done about this, information must be obtained, accurately evaluated, and used for reducing this human tragedy. The armed forces is among the sectors of society in which greatest need of suicide prevention may be evidenced. The possibilities of untapped resources, renewed effectiveness in organization, and mobilized concern, combine to make the study of suicide and attempted suicide a most pressing need.

This chapter will present the clinical research foundation upon which recommendations can be made for effective work with suicidal patients in the armed forces. The design of research will first include subjective, descriptive reports gained through personal interviews with attempted suicide patients in naval hospitals. These reports will be followed by suicide prediction studies which will be evaluated for further armed forces usage. A "Goals of Life" inventory will then be employed, both with attempted suicide patients and a control group, to determine variations in perception of self and others along with certain personality traits and religious dimensions to personality. A "psychological autopsy" study will complete the research procedure by tracing psychological factors involved in cases of armed forces young adults who actually committed suicide. A summary of all findings will conclude the research procedure.

PERSONAL INTERVIEWS

Over a period of approximately three months, from January through March 1970, personal interviews were conducted with twenty active duty military men between seventeen and twenty-five years of age who had actually attempted suicide one or more times. These men were all hospital patients at either Bethesda Naval Hospital in Bethesda, Maryland, or Portsmouth Naval Hospital in Portsmouth, Virginia. The men represent all suicidal patients available during the time of this research in the two hospitals.

Each interview lasted approximately an hour and a half and consisted of three parts. The first part, to be discussed in this section, was the personal response of each patient to six questions asked by this writer. The second part was the rating of suicide risk potential by the writer according to two scales which will be described in the next section of this chapter. The third part was a recording of life goals by each patient as he saw them for himself and others. These were compared with a control group for results, to be described in section three of this chapter.

The first part of the interview took place in an atmosphere of informal conversation as each patient was asked the following six open-ended questions by the interviewer. Notations in parenthesis were not asked, but serve as an indication of what the interviewer was listening for in each of the questions.

TABLE 19
Personal Interview Questions

1. "Tell me a little bit about yourself."—(Rapport, acquaintance, anxiety level, general attitudes, and personal details.)
2. "Could you share with me something of your background?"—(Suicide or mental health problems in family, personal illness, or problem areas, and underlying causes.)
3. "What was occurring in your life just before you came to the hospital?"—(Precipitating causes, nature of relationships, gestures, threats, and methods employed.)
4. "What bearing has being in military service had on your situation?"—(Environmental factors, supportive elements, and effects of loneliness, mobility, and military style of life.)
5. "Is there a particular person or group of persons you've found to be especially helpful to you in this time?"—(Sources of help, forms of assistance, availability of assistance.)
6. "What are your plans and feelings about the future?"—(Role of hope, goals for living, and meaning in life.)

Clinical Findings

Before examining results of the questions, it will be helpful to understand something more of the patients. Among the twenty men, were nineteen Caucasians and one Negro. Their average age was 20.3 years. Eleven were single, seven married, and two separated. Ten were Navy, eight Marine Corps, and two were Army. The average military rank was midpoint between E-2 and E-3, which would be between seaman apprentice and seaman in the Navy or between private first class and lance corporal in the Marine Corps. Sixteen of the men were Protestant, while four were Catholic.

Some significant and rather classic characteristics of the suicidal can already be seen in these descriptions. Their average age of 20.3 years is probably very close to the average age of all men in the armed forces. It testifies both to their youth and to the young age at which suicidal behavior occurs. The age average would very likely be even lower if the hospitals were near one of the Naval Training Centers where recruits are given basic training. San Diego Naval Hospital is in such a position, and reports from there show that 39.2 per cent of the patients with suicidal tendencies are in the lowest grade of E-1.[1] Since the twenty men of this study average only 25 per cent in the E-1 grade, their age average may be higher than the typical suicide patient elsewhere across the services, especially since a reduction in rating has probably occurred.

The ratio of married to single personnel would appear high for men of this age and rank. Including the two separated men, the marriage group comprises 45 per cent of the sample. This might be seen as supporting the one exception to the general population which is typical of young adults. Suicide rates are higher for married rather than single young adults.[2] These men reflect something of that pattern.

The rather high percentage of Marine Corps personnel, 40 per cent of the total twenty patients and 44 per cent of the eighteen representing the Department of the Navy, would tend to comply with Durkheim's theory. He felt the higher percentages of suicide and suicide attempts would be found among elite corps and prestige positions.[3] Since the Marine Corps would represent only about 35 per cent of the naval establishment, 44 per cent would seem to be a high portion of suicidal patients.[4]

The rank or rate average of these twenty patients is perhaps indicative not only of their youth, but of their lack of ability to accomplish work well. This would appear to confirm other military studies of the suicidal which show, unlike college students, that military personnel have difficulty in accomplishing their work.

And, here again, we see the Protestant propensity to suicide with Catholics in the minority. The four to one ratio is probably double what the population religious preference would indicate if suicidal behavior were the same across faith groups.[5] The fact that three of the four Catholics were also Marines, gives sharper focus to the elite factor. Without it, the religious picture might be even more extreme, as indeed, general population studies so indicate.

A wide variety of responses came from the twenty men while replying informally to the six question areas. In tables to follow, it shall be our purpose to simply hold up the several areas which the men chose to emphasize most strongly. Numbers will indicate how many responded in similar fashion. In these open-ended questions, no attempt was made to elicit from each man a similar or dissimilar response to the items listed. The responses, therefore, represent descriptive portrayal rather than statistical measurement. A complete listing of responses may be viewed in Appendix A.

TABLE 20

Tell Me a Little Bit About Yourself
Question Number One

Responses	Number
Likes sports	5
Makes friends easily	4
Doesn't make friends easily	4
Confused	4
Likes music	3
Depressed	3
Moody	3
Family trouble	3

As a group, the men would appear in this first question to be ambivalent in their own emotions and relationships with others. Their word "confused" may be most descriptive of themselves.

Clinical Findings 83

This may be further indicated by the fact that five was the largest number of like feelings on any subject. The interest expressed in both sports and music, along with friendship, perhaps substantiates the research saying depression is not the chief characteristic of military suicide patients.

TABLE 21

Could You Share With Me Something
of Your Background?
Question Number Two

Responses	*Number*
Meaningful mention of father	12
Poor health	9
Broken home	7
Finished high school	5
Didn't finish high school	5
Oldest child	5
Good health	4

Answers to this question appear to support those studies emphasizing the importance of the father relationship to suicidal patients, especially men. Not only was father mentioned more often than any other subject discussed in question two, but he was usually spoken of immediately and in regard to traumatic, lonely, or disappointing experiences.

After father, the patient's own poor health is most often discussed. This centered primarily on poor physical health concerns within the previous year, but in many cases did extend back to earliest years. This concern parallels those expressed in studies which rate physical health of chief importance to male suicidal patients.

Broken homes were often mentioned in connection with the discussion of fathers. While not referred to as often as fathers, the broken home theme usually seemed to carry more emotional weight.

Half of the men cared to mention school work, with the interesting fifty-fifty split at five each for finishing and not finishing. One might posit that school and education do loom as significant for about half the men, with some concerned that they didn't finish and some feeling a definite need to "prove" to the interviewer that they did.

Twenty-five per cent mentioned they were the oldest child of the family, and others may have been. The mentioned number alone would seem to add weight to the oldest or youngest child theories of suicidal behavior. Only one man, however, expressed that he was the youngest child.

No brief phrase or number figure can reflect the emotion most of the patients exhibited in dealing with question three (Table 22 which follows). For many, it appeared they might not be able to complete the interview, but all did. As can be seen in the Table, the number of responses were as high and as concentrated as any in the study.

TABLE 22

What Was Occurring in Your Life Just
Before You Came to the Hospital?
Question Number Three

Responses	Number
Took pills	12
Girl friend or family worry	11
Previous attempt	10
Attempt made after 6:00 P.M.	8
Military trouble	6
Depressed	6
Cut wrist	6
Attempt made before noon	6
Wanted to kill self	5
Attempt in January	5
Debts	4
Previous hospitalization	4

Pills, at the head of the list, show the attempt rather than commit tendency in these patients. Not one of the twenty reported use of firearms or explosives. Such violent methods are usually used, as statistics indicate, by those who are not available for later interview.

The intimate relationships of family and girl friends are particularly stressful concerns of these patients. This is not to say they are involved in many outgoing relationships, but that the primary

Clinical Findings

ones are much on their thoughts as causes of concern. From a mother's operation to a girl friend who's seeing another man, personal trauma in these intimate relations appears all important.

The fact that 50 per cent mentioned a previous attempt should cause an extra flag of concern to be raised. This factor is reported by many as the key indicator of possible completed suicide in the future. Low as these patients may score on other actual suicide indicators, this one indicator alone means their situation cannot be treated at all lightly.

The weight of occurrence after evening hours again indicates the attempt rather than actual suicide pattern according to those who say suicide is a daytime, working hours activity.

Several of the items of question three can and probably should be considered together. Family and girl friend move very quickly to debts, depressed, wanted to kill self, military trouble, and cut wrist. There's an almost typical sequence to be seen in these few words. The chain reaction syndrome should be noted, that at some point it could hopefully be shifted in a more positive and hopeful cycle.

The attempt rate mentioned in January may show the winter month attempt, rather than commit feature researchers claim, but it probably also is related to the time this study was conducted. Patients are in Naval Hospitals only briefly with these problems; and January was just before this research.

The reactions of all men except two (in Table 23) were

TABLE 23

What Bearing has being in Military Service
Had on Your Situation?
Question Number Four

Responses	Number
Military schedule ruined family	6
Military messed him up	4
More pressure	4
Don't want to be in military	3
Can't stand it	3
Scared (trouble)	3
Caused debts	3

negative about the bearing of military service on their problems. Yet, most responses were rather vague and wandering. The clearest reaction was the highest scoring one regarding service life and schedule ruining the family. Family here includes parents, wife, or fiance. Many other responses were related to this one. A fairly typical response came from one man who said he's been away from his wife for 85 per cent of the last three years.

The three responses—"military messed him up," "can't stand it," and "don't want to be in the military" are all closely related. They remind one of the study by Tucker and Reinhardt (also with Naval personnel) in which 73 per cent of their suicidal patients initially said, "Let me out."[6] In this study, the expressions covered wide varieties of upsets, failures, disappointments, and hostility.

The response of "scared" was a bit curious. Several seemed to feel they were going to cause trouble, have others get them in trouble, or simply that unknowns were going to bring about difficulties.

Debts, mentioned in connection with families, represent the most concrete item of upset for which the patient holds the military environment responsible. This correlates in some fashion with the responses from question three which also referred to debts as a problem prior to hospitalization.

All responses were recorded to question five (Table 24) to show both the variety and significance. Fully 50 per cent say when the cry for help goes out there is "no one." This may demonstrate both the "loner" characteristics of the suicidal and the insensitive nature of those around him. Apparently, the closest people on the job may be the first to respond as indicated in "working supervisor." The chaplain is mentioned next and if minister and priest might be added one could say, from this study, that clergymen are initially turned to and provide help to the suicidal twice as often as any other person or group. The surprise is that no patient mentioned wife, mother, or father as a source of help.

Most of the men (referred to in Table 25) had positive, firm feelings for future plans. Only one man said flatly, "no future." Work, school, and family relationships were the most obvious concerns for most patients. Again, it's interesting to note

TABLE 24

Is There A Particular Person or Group of Persons You've Found to Be Especially Helpful To You in This Time?
Question Number Five

Responses	Number
No one	10
Working supervisor	2
Chaplain	2
Doctor	1
Commanding officer	1
Psychiatrist	1
Neighbors	1
Minister	1
Fellow patients	1
Priest	1
Lawyer	1

TABLE 25

What are your Plans and Feelings About the Future?
Question Number Six

Responses	Number
Work	6
College or school	6
Discharge	4
Catch up on bills	4
Provide for family	3
Try to be something	3
Travel	3

the reference to bills, particularly if coupled with the following category of "provide for family." Several knew they wanted to do well at something and have a good life regardless of specific plans. Others simply wanted time to travel and reflect on who they were, and what life was all about for them.

A summary and evaluation of findings from all six subjective questions will be presented in the last section of this chapter.

SUICIDE POTENTIAL RATINGS

After the personal interview, two suicide potential rating scales were completed with information gained from the interview and additional questions. These potential rating scales were used to see if they would give meaningful estimates of a patient's future suicide risk, and to see if a similar revised scale could be suggested for use with disturbed military personnel.

The "Suicidal Potential Evaluation" is a prediction scale used by the Contra Costa Suicide Prevention Center of Walnut

TABLE 26
Suicidal Potential Evaluation

(Callers scoring "yes" to 7 or more are high risks as potential suicides).

1. Is this person *male?*
2. Is this person *white?*
3. Is this person *45 years of age or older?*
4. Is this person *separated, divorced,* or *widowed?*
5. Is this person *retired or unemployed?*
6. Is this person presently *living alone?*
7. Is this person at present address less than 6 months? Transient ——
8. Has this person *attempted suicide before?* (Now in process.)
9. Is the person unconscious or *unable to answer coherently* as a result of the present suicide attempt?
10. Has this person had a *previous psychiatric hospitalization?*
11. Was this person *in poor health* during the past 6 months?
12. Did this person *write a suicide* note at this present attempt?
13. Does this person now have, or has he ever had, a problem with *alcohol?*
14. *Drug addiction?*
15. *Homosexuality?*
16. The *law?*
17. *Illegitimacy?*
18. Has this person suffered a *loss—real, threatened or fantasied—*within the last six months (e.g., death, separation, financial, self-esteem, etc.)?
19. Did this person *come from a broken home* (death or separation from one or both parents before the age of 16)?

Clinical Findings

Creek, California.[7] This scale is used primarily by telephone volunteers in assessing the "lethality" of callers who telephone in from the general population with suicidal feelings. Note that a rating of seven or more positive replies out of nineteen is considered as high risk.

Table 27 shows the responses of the twenty suicide patients in terms of how many gave "yes" answers to the questions. According to this record of responses only three men out of the twenty could be considered high risk based on this scale.

TABLE 27

Positive Replies to Suicidal Potential Evaluation

Number of men	Number of "yes" responses
1	2
4	3
2	4
4	5
6	6
1	7
2	8
Total men 20	

Table 28 shows exactly which questions the men gave their "yes" answers to and how many went to each question.

TABLE 28

Positive Replies to Suicidal Potential Evaluation by Question

Question	Number of "yes" responses
1. Male	20
2. White	19
3. 45 years of age or older	0
4. Separated, divorced, or widowed	2
5. Retired or unemployed	0

Question	Number of "yes" responses
6. Living alone	2
7. Transient	4
8. Attempted suicide before	10
9. Unable to answer coherently	0
10. Previous psychiatric hospitalization	4
11. In poor health	8
12. Write a suicide note	3
13. Alcohol	1
14. Drug addiction	3
15. Homosexuality	1
16. The law	4
17. Illegitimacy	0
18. Loss—real, threatened, or fantasied	14
19. Come from a broken home	8

Obviously, the "male" and "white" question gave virtually an automatic start with two "yes" responses. In previous discussions, however, the great importance of these two factors in suicide occurrence has been delineated. The high "yes" response to question eighteen is particularly worthy of note. Fourteen of the twenty men had suffered a traumatic personal loss of loved one or loss of self-esteem within the previous six months.

The second prediction scale is one evolved by Jacob Tuckman and William F. Youngman as a "High and Low Risk Category" study. This scale was developed while working with the records of 3,800 attempted suicide cases on file in the Philadelphia Police Department.[8] The numbers listed under "Suicide rate" indicate the actual recorded suicide rate per 1,000 population, which occurred for the risk factor among the 3,800 suicides (see Table 29). This shows the statistical validity for selection and rank of these factors as indicators of potential suicide risk.

Factor	High-risk category	Suicide rate	Low-risk category	Suicide rate
Age	45 years of age and older	24.0	Under 45 years of age	9.4
Sex	Male	19.9	Female	9.2
Race	White	14.3	Nonwhite	8.7
Marital status	Separated, divorced, widowed	12.5	Single, Married	8.6
Living arrangements	Alone	48.4	With others	10.1
Employment status	Unemployed, retired	16.8	Employed	14.3
Physical health	Poor (acute or chronic condition in the 6 month period preceding the attempt)	14.0	Good	12.4
Mental condition	Nervous or mental disorder, mood or behavioral symptoms including alcoholism	19.1	Presumably normal including brief situational reactions	7.2
Medical care (within 6 months)	Yes	16.4	No	10.8
Method	Hanging, firearms, jumping, drowning	28.4	Cutting or piercing, gas or carbon monoxide, poison, combination of other methods, other	12.0
Season	Warm months (April to September)	14.2	Cold months (October to March)	10.9
Time of day	6:00 A.M.-5:59 P.M.	15.1	6:00 P.M.-5:59 A.M.	10.5
Where attempt was made	Own or someone else's home	14.3	Other type of premises, out-of-doors	11.9
Time interval between attempt and discovery	Almost immediately reported by person making attempt	10.9	Later	7.2
Intent to kill (self-report)	No	14.5	Yes	8.5
Suicide note	Yes	16.7	No	12.3
Previous attempt or threat	Yes	25.2	No	11.0

*Jacob Tuckman and William F. Youngman, "A Scale For Assessing Suicide Risk of Attempted Suicides," Clinical Psychology XXIV No. 1 (January, 1968), pp. 17-23.

While the first scale is used by a Suicide Prevention Center to judge lethality of those who may attempt suicide, this second scale is designed to determine whether or not attempters are likely to go on to commit suicide. A score of six or more in the high risk column is considered high risk potential.

Table 30 shows all responses to the seventeen items of the "High and Low Category" scale, divided into two columns—the one showing high scores, the other low.

TABLE 30

Responses to High Risk–Low Risk Category Scale

Factor	High Risk	Low Risk
Age	0	20
Sex	20	0
Race	19	1
Marital status	2	18
Living arrangements	2	18
Employment status	0	20
Physical health	6	14
Mental condition	10	10
Medical care	12	8
Method	1	19
Season	1	19
Time of day	8	12
Where attempted	14	5
Time interval between attempt and discovery	16	4
Intent to kill (self report)	6	14
Suicide note	3	17
Previous attempt or threat	10	10

The men scored highest risk as a group on the factors of sex, race, recent medical care, attempt made in home or barracks, and little time interval between attempt and discovery or report. Lowest risk items included age, the fact they were employed, the season of occurrence, and the methods employed. The two categories receiving exactly equal response were mental condition and previous attempt or threat. Fifty per cent difficulty in these areas would appear to warrant extra cause for alarm.

That alarm is registered most dramatically in Figure 4 which

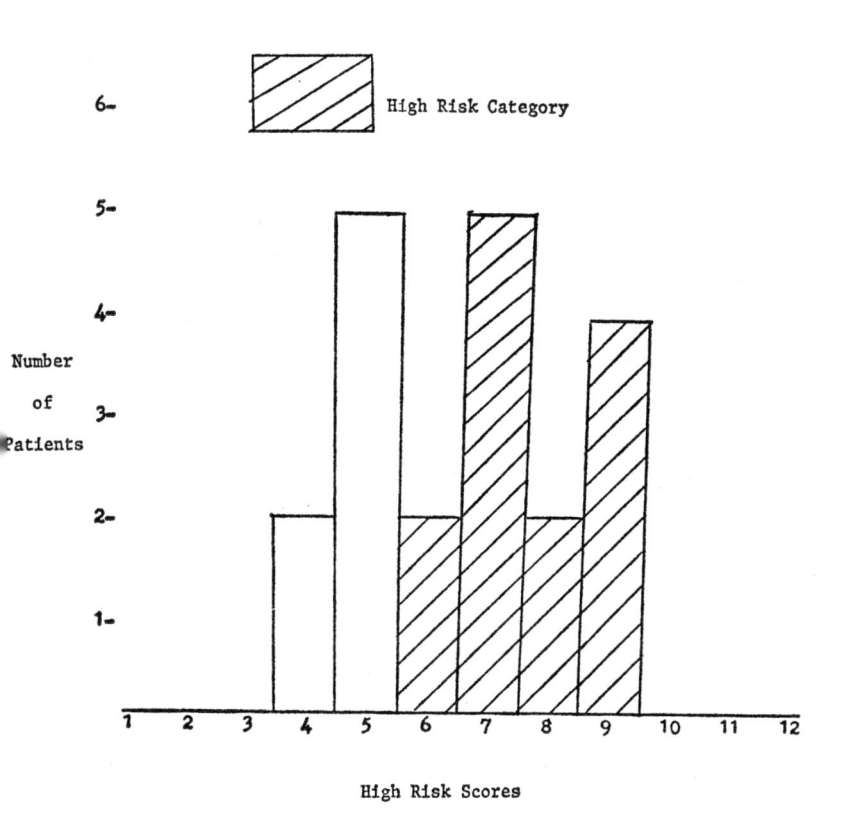

FIGURE 4.—Results High Risk Category Positive Responses

shows how many men registered in high as compared to low risk categories. According to the calculations made by Tuckman and Youngman, six to nine checks on the high risk side would equal a suicide rate, based on their study of 3,800 suicide attempts, of 19.61 per 1,000 population of previous attempters. That is, with six to nine checks in the high risk list, 19.61 persons of a group of 1,000 suicide attempt patients could be expected to go on to actual completion of suicide.[9]

This prediction scale indicates only seven of the twenty men could be considered a low risk, or 6.98 per 1,000 completion predictability, while thirteen of them would be high risk and expect to complete the suicidal act on a scale of 19.61 per 1,000. The four men ranking nine high risk scores would appear to be at the peak of this high risk range. No one scored over nine to place in the extremely high range of 60.61 per 1,000, based on a possible of ten to twelve high risk checks.

The difference between the three who rated high potential on the first scale and the thirteen who rated high risk on the second will be evaluated along with a summary of evaluation scales in the concluding section of the chapter.

GOALS OF LIFE INVENTORY

When the suicidal potential and high risk scales were completed, each suicide patient was asked to work on a "Goals of Life" Inventory. The inventory is the same as used by Robert Lawrence Carrigan in his 1962 Union Theological Seminary Th.D. thesis in which ulcerative colitis patients were compared with orthopedic patients to discern variations in goals of life.[10] The inventory places special emphasis upon the religious dimension of personality, while evaluating other facets of personality and life's goals. The patient is asked to rank sixteen goals of life by number with one as the most important and sixteen the least important. The ranking is first done on the basis of how the patient thinks "other" people would rank them in importance. The patient then ranks each of the same sixteen items as he himself feels they are important in his life. A concluding rating scale of the questions themselves offers the patient opportunity to indicate agreement, disagreement, neutral or various in be-

Clinical Findings

tween opinions as to the validity of each question serving as a goal of life.

The same "Goals of Life" Inventory was used with a control group of twenty military general medical patients on surgery and orthopedic wards. These patients were randomly selected and matched with the suicide sample group in age, sex, race, active duty status, and general level of military enlisted rank. Both sample and control group averaged about twenty years of age. They were all male. Each group had one Negro and the rest Caucasians. All members were active duty military personnel and both groups averaged approximately the E-3 level of military rank.

The inventory was completed by all patients in accordance with the directions on its first page. A list of the "Goals of Life" will be found in Table 31. The complete inventory with its directions, lists of goals, and rating of questions appears in Appendix B.

TABLE 31

Goals of Life

A. Self-sacrifice for the sake of a better world; giving oneself for others.
B. Peace of mind, contentment, quietness of spirit.
C. Serving the community of which one is a part.
D. Devotion to God, doing God's will.
E. Being genuinely concerned about other people.
F. Finding one's place in life and accepting it.
G. Achieving personal life after death; going to heaven.
H. Discovering a way of personal communion with God.
I. Making a place for oneself in the world; getting ahead.
J. Doing one's duty.
K. Being able to "take it"; brave and uncomplaining acceptance of what life brings.
L. Giving love and security to one's family.
M. Understanding oneself; having a mature outlook.
N. Depending on a personal message from God.
O. Disciplining oneself to a wholesome and clean way of life.
P. Participating fully in the life and work of the church.

Table 32 presents the median score and median rank of all sixteen statements as both the sample and control group rates them for "self." The median was selected for placement rather than the mean, as the 50 per cent above and 50 per cent below designation tends to avoid an average that moves toward the extremes. Median rank of each statement was obtained by positing one for the lowest median score and proceeding up to sixteen with half ranks accorded to tieing scores.

TABLE 32

Median Score and Rank for "Self"

Sample Group Median Rank	Median Score	Life-Goals*	Control Group Median Score	Median Rank
7.5	8	A	9.5	11.5
2	4	B	5.5	2.5
16	12.5	C	10.5	14
4	6.5	D	5	1
7.5	8	E	10	13
12.5	11	F	6.5	5
9	9	G	9	10
12.5	11	H	7.5	7
5.5	7	I	6	4
11	10	J	8.5	9
14	11.5	K	8	8
1	3	L	5.5	2.5
3	6	M	7	6
15	12	N	14	16
5.5	7	O	9.5	11.5
10	9.5	P	13	15

S-Group	L	B	M	D	O	I	A	E	G	P	J	F	H	K	N	C
Comparative	1	2	3	4	5	6	7	8	9	10	11	12	13	14	15	16
Rankings	1	2	3	4	5	6	7	8	9	10	11	12	13	14	15	16
C-Group	D	B	L	I	F	M	H	K	J	G	O	A	E	C	P	N

*See Table 31.

The highest ranking statement for the suicide group was "L"—"Giving love and security to one's family," implying, per-

Clinical Findings

haps, that they wanted to achieve in their family of the present and future what had been painfully lacking in the past. The control group also ranked this high at 2.5.

Highest ranking for the control group went to "D"—"Devotion to God, doing God's Will." With this life and personal affairs more in order, the control group could possibly find itself more capable of reaching beyond self. This concern is fairly strong with the suicide group, however, since they accorded "D" a rank of four.

The sixteenth ranking statement for the suicide group was "C"—"Serving the community of which one is a part." The suicidal patient probably doesn't feel part of any community, and therefore feels incapable of serving one. It is interesting to note, however, that the control group rates this as low as fourteen too.

Because of the control group's first place choice, it might seem strange that they rank "N" in last place in number sixteen —"Depending on a personal message from God." This could be taken to mean that while they want to do His will, they don't expect an inside mystical track to supernatural knowledge.

Both groups rank "B" high, at two for the suicide, sample or S-group and 2.5 for the control or C-group. "Peace of mind, contentment, quietness of spirit" is apparently a major quest of the young patient amid today's turbulent world.

Statement "G"—"Achieving personal life after death; going to heaven," shows the greatest consistency in score and rank in both group ratings. It falls just below the midpoint at nine and ten.

The largest differences between how the S-group sees its goals and the C-group sees its own, appears in statements "E," "F," "H," "K," and "C." The widest disparity of these five differences occurs in "F"—"Finding one's place in life and accepting it." The S-group ranks this at 12.5 while the C-group gives it a five. The suicide patients have perhaps found little place in life, and the little they've experienced may have seemed unacceptable. The response to item "K" may be related. The S-group gives fourteen and the C-group eight to "Being able to 'take it' brave and uncomplaining acceptance of what life brings." Suicide patients may feel they've already taken it and have little desire to brave more. Items "E," "H," and "O" show the S-group again demonstrating more interest in getting along with people than with God and perhaps thinking they can do so by "O"—"Disciplining oneself to a wholesome and clean way of life."

Table 33 shows the median score and rank for the sixteen goals as both the S-group and C-group rank them for "others." This is how they think others would rank these goals.

TABLE 33
Median Score and Rank for "Others"

Sample Group		Life-Goals*	Control Group	
Median Rank	Median Score		Median Score	Median Rank
13	11	A	8	8.5
3	5.5	B	7	5.5
5.5	6.5	C	9	11
5.5	6.5	D	7.5	7
14.5	11.5	E	13	15
2	5	F	4.5	3
10	9.5	G	10.5	13
9	9	H	9.5	12
1	2	I	4	2
7	7.5	J	6.5	4
14.5	11.5	K	7	5.5
4	6	L	3.5	1
8	8	M	8	8.5
16	12.5	N	13.5	16
12	10.5	O	8.5	10
11	10	P	12	14

S-Group	I	F	B	L	C	D	J	M	H	G	P	O	A	E	K	N
Comparative	1	2	3	4	5	6	7	8	9	10	11	12	13	14	15	16
Rankings	1	2	3	4	5	6	7	8	9	10	11	12	13	14	15	16
C-Group	L	I	F	J	B	K	D	M	A	O	C	H	G	P	E	N

*See Table 31, p. 95.

There is an amazing similarity in how both the S-group and C-group rank the goals for others. Both rank "I"—"Making a place for oneself in the world; getting ahead," right at the top, with the S-group giving it first place and the C-group ranking it second. Others are apparently seen as scrambling to "make it."

Clinical Findings

Complete agreement was obtained on last place. Both groups give sixteenth ranking to "N"—"Depending on a personal message from God." This statement seems to regularly carry a negative connotation.

The two places of disparity were items "C" and "K." The S-group gave a 5.5 ranking to "C"—"Serving the community of which one is a part," while the C-group ranked it in eleventh place. Suicidal patients may think others care about the community more than they do, while C-group patients doubt it. Considerable disparity shows on "K"—"Being able to 'take it' brave and uncomplaining acceptance of what life brings." The S-group ranked it down to 14.5 and the C-group gave it 5.5. This goal of life is apparently difficult for the S-group to attribute to themselves or others.

Table 34 brings together the median scores for both "self" and "others" as both the S-group and C-group rated them. This provides the oportunity of determining how much disparity there is between how both groups see themselves in comparison with how they see others.

TABLE 34
Median Score for "Self" and "Others"

Sample Group Median Score		Life-Goals*	Control Group Median Score	
"Others"	"Self"		"Self"	"Others"
11	8	A	9.5	8
5.5	4	B	5.5	7
6.5	12.5	C	10.5	9
6.5	6.5	D	5	7.5
11.5	8	E	10	13
5	11	F	6.5	4.5
9.5	9	G	9	10.5
9	11	H	7.5	9.5
2	7	I	6	4
7.5	10	J	8.5	6.5
11.5	11.5	K	8	7
6	3	L	5.5	3.5
8	6	M	7	8
12.5	12	N	14	13.5
10.5	7	O	9.5	8.5
10	9.5	P	13	12

*See Table 31.

The Spearman Rank Correlation Coefficient was applied in determining the level of correlation between the ranking of "self" goals and "others" goals of both the C-group and S-group.[11] This statistic, sometimes called "rho," is obtained by determining the difference (d_i) between two ranked items, squaring that number (d_i^2), obtaining the sum of differences squared (Σ), multiplied by six, and divided by the number of the questions (N) cubed, minus the number of questions; which can be worked through this formula to determine "rho" or the degree of correlation.

$$\text{rho } (r_s) = 1 - \frac{6 \sum_{i=1}^{N} d_i^2}{N^3 - N}$$

For the Sample group the following level of significance was obtained:

$$\Sigma d_i^2 = 149.75$$

$$\text{rho} = 1 - \frac{6(149.75)}{16^3 - 16} = 0.782$$

Significant at the 0.01 level

The Control group significance was:

$$\Sigma d_i^2 = 50.5$$

$$\text{rho} = 1 - \frac{6(50.5)}{16^3 - 16} = 0.926$$

Significant at the 0.01 level

Both scores show a high level of correlation but the Sample group shows a greater level of disparity between how they view "others" goals and their own, i.e., suicidal patients are more inclined to see themselves as different from others.

From Table 34 it can be seen that the level of disparity be-

Clinical Findings 101

tween views of self and others was quite low in the C-group. The biggest difference in median scores is only three points on item "E"—"Being genuinely concerned about other people." The C-group ranked this ten for themselves and thirteen for others, both of which fall in relatively low categories.

However, three items show quite significant levels of disparity in the S-group ranking for self and others. Statements "C," "F," and "I" are rated relatively high for others and low for oneself. A score of 6.5 is given for others and 12.5 for self on "C"—"Serving the community of which one is a part." "F"—"Finding one's place in life and accepting it," received five for others and eleven for self. "I"—"Making a place for oneself in the world; getting ahead," received two for others and seven for self.

Carrigan, in his thesis, attributes certain meanings to the various statements.[12] He would say that "C" and "I" represent orientation toward "Action" or action-imperatives, which the suicidal patient does not see in himself as compared to others. Perhaps he feels he has already passed that stage and is looking for something else. He may feel that action is impossible or futile when attempted. Carrigan sees "F" as orientation toward "Personality focus." The suicidal is not as interested as he thinks others may be in that personality development which depends on "accepting it" as a feature of finding one's place.

Table 35 is an intensity rating of how the two groups responded to the goals themselves. Following Carrigan's pattern, the statements are grouped as they reflect Passivity (A, B, G, K, N), Activity (C, I, J, P), "High" religious (D, E, F, P), or Self-indulgent (F, G, I, H) characteristics.[13] The "Sign Test" is applied by pairs whereby plus and minus signs are established, based on a greater or lesser response by the Sample Group as compared to the Control group to any statement in one of the four groups. The minus signs are then divided by the total number of plus and minus signs (omitting O or equal responses), and from this figure the level of significance may be determined by reference to a Table of Probabilities.[14] As can be seen, none of the tests achieved a level of significance of 0.05; and, therefore, we can conclude that both groups are basically the same in these four characteristics, and show no significant differences.

TABLE 35
Life Goals Intensity Rating

	Test of Passivity (A, B, G, K, N)				Test of Activity (C, I, J, P)		
Pairs	S-Group	C-Group	Sign	Pairs	S-Group	C-Group	Sign
1	3	2	−	1	2	3	−
2	4	1	+	2	0	3	−
3	2	2	0	3	0	1	−
4	2	4	−	4	0	2	−
5	3	5	−	5	3	3	0
6	1	2	−	6	2	2	0
7	2	1	+	7	3	1	+
8	3	2	+	8	2	1	+
9	4	1	+	9	3	1	+
10	2	2	0	10	2	2	0
11	2	2	0	11	1	2	−
12	3	0	+	12	3	1	+
13	3	3	0	13	0	2	−
14	1	4	−	14	2	1	+
15	2	4	−	15	3	3	0
16	2	4	−	16	0	1	−
17	2	2	0	17	1	2	−
18	2	3	−	18	3	4	−
19	3	1	+	19	2	2	0
20	1	0	+	20	1	1	0
Totals	47	45	8+	Totals	34	37	5+
			7−				9−

A rating of 1 is a low passivity response; a 5 rating is a high passivity response.
Level of significance = 0.05
Probability of 7/15 = 0.500*

Conclusion—No significant difference between S-group and C-group

A rating of 1 is low activity; a 4 rating is a high activity response
Level of significance = 0.05
Probability of 5/14 = 0.212*

(Note the pluses were used to determine the probability because they were the sign of the least number.)

Conclusion—No significant difference between S-group and C-group.

Clinical Findings

	Test of "high" religious goals (D, E, H, P)				Test of self-indulgent goals (F, G, I, N)		
Pairs	S-Group	C-Group	Sign	Pairs	S-Group	C-Group	Sign
1	3	3	0	1	4	2	+
2	1	1	0	2	2	2	0
3	3	1	+	3	1	0	+
4	2	3	−	4	0	4	−
5	4	4	0	5	4	3	+
6	0	1	−	6	1	1	0
7	1	2	−	7	1	3	−
8	1	1	0	8	3	4	−
9	4	1	+	9	3	2	+
10	1	1	0	10	2	2	0
11	2	0	+	11	2	2	0
12	2	1	+	12	4	1	+
13	3	0	+	13	2	2	0
14	0	2	−	14	2	1	+
15	2	4	−	15	1	3	−
16	1	2	−	16	2	2	0
17	2	2	0	17	3	1	+
18	2	4	−	18	2	3	−
19	4	2	+	19	3	2	+
20	2	1	+	20	3	1	+
Totals	40	36	7+	Totals	45	41	9+
			7−				5−

A rating of one is a low religiosity response; a four rating is a high response.
Level of significance = 0.05
Probability of 7/14 = 0.605*

Conclusion—No significant difference between S-group and C-group.

A rating of one is less self-indulgent; a four rating is more self-indulgent.
Level of significance = 0.05
Probability of 5/14 = 0.212*

Conclusion—No significant difference between S-group and C-group.

---

*Siegel, *Nonparametric Statistics for the Behavioral Sciences*, p. 250.

PSYCHOLOGICAL AUTOPSIES

The "Psychological Autopsy" is a procedure developed in recent years by Shneidman, Farberow, and associates of the Los Angeles Suicide Prevention Center.[15] By a review of the social, emotional, and psychological factors involved in a committed suicide, they found that is was possible to gather important clues in understanding suicidal motives and characteristics.

This section of "Clinical Findings" is a study in the form of psychological autopsies, conducted in a review of records from Bethesda Naval Hospital for the last five years. During that time, four young adult servicemen took their own lives while attached to the hospital as patients. Three men were Caucasian, one was Negro. Three men were enlisted, one was an officer. Three were Protestant, one was Catholic. All four were single. Three of the suicides occured in the high risk season of February, March, and April. The fourth occured in July, after an attempt in the earlier high risk season. Three of the suicides took place in the morning hours before noon, the fourth occurred in the afternoon during working hours. Several of the traditional high risk characteristics can already be noted; now for an individual examination.

Patient "A," born in the 1930's, was found by his brother shot in the chest on a late spring afternoon of the mid 1960's. Death occurred in the patient's bedroom of the family home, located in a large city. The patient was on authorized liberty from Bethesda Naval Hospital at the time of his death. He was scheduled to be released from the hospital the next day had he not committed suicide.

Patient "A" was a single Negro, Catholic, Navy enlisted man. He was under investigation at the time of his death by the Office of Naval Intelligence for circumstances falling within the realm of SECNAV INST. 1900.9, "Policy and Procedures for the Separation of Members of the Naval Service by Reason of Homosexuality."

Prior to his death, Patient "A" had been admitted to the hospital for a glandular swelling diagnosed as mumps. No psychiatric evaluation had been made.

Clinical Findings

The brother of Patient "A" was also in the house and rushed to the upper part of the home when he heard gunshots. Patient "A" was found with the revolver on the bed, which belonged to his father. The autopsy established that death was caused by a gunshot wound to the heart.

Patient "A" was reported to have expressed to his family that he thought he was suffering from a blood disease similar to, if not in fact, leukemia. Medical records showed nothing of this nor of any unusual condition during the patient's hospitalization.

Factors which should be noted as important clues to causation are: fear of physical impairment, and use of father's gun along with homosexuality charge, indicating manhood conflicts in relationship to the father. The gun, bedroom location, times of year and day, are also factors supporting suicide completion motive. The unlikely combination for suicide, of Negro and Catholic, may reflect more of an identity problem than anything else.

Patient "B," born in the early 1940's, was found dead from shotgun wounds on an early spring morning of the mid 1960's. Death occured in a public park adjacent to a large city. The patient was on authorized liberty from the hospital, and was due to see his doctor the morning after his suicide, for the last appointment prior to a 30 per cent medical disability discharge because of a neurotic depressive reaction.

Patient "B" was a single, Caucasian, Protestant, Navy junior officer. He had been hopitalized for sometime due to the depressive reaction. Hospital care was also rendered the year before for a previous suicide attempt by self-inflicted stab wounds.

The month before his death, Patient "B" had liquidated his stocks and prepared his Last Will and Testament.

Patient "B" was considered to be a perfectionist. His academic achievements were among the highest in the naval service. As an instructor, he was considered outstanding. Yet, there was evidence he was not satisfied with his own accomplishment.

The father of Patient "B" had criticized him and insisted on exemplary behavior. The patient was also the first born son. A younger brother had previously attempted suicide in the Air Force. The father died of a heart attack when Patient "B" was eleven years old. After that the patient attended the same schools as his father right through college years.

Death came to Patient "B" in the early morning hours by way of a twelve-gauge shotgun. The barrel was placed in his mouth and discharged. Several suicide notes were sent to relatives prior to the act.

Again, one should note the father-relationship factor, the perfectionist drive that undermined accomplishment, the mental illness, the use of a shotgun, and the crucial timing—both seasonal and at the climax of hospitalization.

Patient "C," born in the late 1940's, was the victim of an overdose of Darvon Compound, taken in the barracks on an early spring morning of the late 1960's.

Patient "C" was a single, Caucasian, Protestant, Navy enlisted man. He had been admitted to the hospital the month before because of an overdosage of pills, at which time he explained his action as, "being fed up with regulations, uniformity, triviality of military life," and said he wanted to "get out of the whole rat race."

The background of Patient "C" indicates he was the oldest of three children and related more to his mother than to "his rather cold and reserved father." His adolescence was marked by good grades, loneliness, and daydreaming. College ended in fiasco due to lack of direction and disappointment in love. His service record had been satisfactory.

During the previous suicide attempt hospitalization, Patient "C" did not appear depressed, but rather emotionally immature.

A review of this situation reminds one of manipulative suicide, or perhaps simply attempted suicide that went too far. Classic factors are present such as oldest child, poor father relationship, lonely youth, immature, and "wants to get out." The prior attempt should have served as a strong alarm signal.

Patient "D," born in the early 1950's, was found dead in his car on an early summer morning, the victim of a self-inflicted gunshot wound. He was on authorized liberty from the hospital, where he was undergoing psychiatric treatment.

Patient "D" was a single, Caucasian, Protestant, Marine enlisted man. Unknown to the Marine Corps, he had received psychiatric assistance before coming into the military, and had been receiving psychiatric help in the military almost from the time he first enlisted. At one point in treatment he was known to say

Clinical Findings

that he had enlisted in the military because he "wanted to die." He had once reported that he had been messed up all his life. He was the seventh of eight brothers in a family with a chronic alcoholic father. Patient "D" had been a nervous child, had little social life, and was often found by himself daydreaming.

In a previous suicide attempt, Patient "D" had ingested 100 aspirin. This occurred about the time his older brother joined the Marine Corps.

Patient "D" was found shot to death, slumped over behind the steering wheel of his brother's car. The wound had been inflicted to the head by a newly purchased rifle bought the day before by the deceased.

One has a feeling of seeing an especially tragic life in reviewing factors pertaining to Patient "D." Mental illness had been long-term. Home life must have been a constant nightmare. The only strength came from an older brother who left him, and in retaliation the victim took his own life in the brother's car. The previous attempt, along with illness and general attitude, should have constantly marked this man as an extremely high risk.

Several factors stand out in these four cases beyond the initial ones mentioned. All four had difficult relationships with their fathers. Three of the four died by gunshot wounds. Three had made a previous attempt. All had been hospitalized, and two of the four were due to leave the hospital imminently. Only one left a suicide note. Two were the oldest child, and a third was of unknown sibling placement, and the fourth was nearly the youngest of a large family.

SUMMARY AND EVALUATION OF THE FINDINGS

Now, going back to the beginning of this chapter, summary will first be offered covering the interviews with twenty suicide patients. These subjective personal interviews based on the six questions of Table 19 pointed to some significant areas of importance in understanding suicidal behavior among these military young adults. The first factor to be noted was the disturbance in family life for the suicidal patient. He tended to come from a broken home, a traumatic parental relationship, or a deprived situation in terms of loss of a love object. Much of this general disturbance appeared to carry over into married life as well.

Military life at its most rigorous phases seemed to be the second factor of major distress to these people. Long separations, continued hardship tours, impersonal attitude of superiors and associates, and lack of understanding or assistance with personal problems weighed heavily upon the concern of the suicidal. These factors often combined with the poor family relationships to cause upset and frantic manipulative appeals saying, "Let me out."

On top of these basic factors, additional stress was often added because of indebtedness as the result of low pay for married enlisted personnel in the lowest pay grades (nine of the twenty were married).

When the moment of breakdown approached, half the men could turn to no one for help, either because of their personality or failure of others to pick up clues and respond to them. Clergymen and fellow workers close at hand were among those most often helpful. Some applications of these and other summary evaluations will be offered in the final chapter.

The two suicide prediction scales appeared helpful in determining suicide risks, though their results differed widely. The scale by Tuckman and Youngman, evaluating the high and low risk categories of those who'd already attempted suicide once, seemed the most appropriate and helpful for military young adult suicide patients. By this scale, thirteen of the twenty men ranked in the high risk category as compared to only three in the other suicide potential rating. Tuckman and Youngman included six categories on their scale, which were not on the Contra Costa scale, and which most suicidology literature considers important. They are: mental condition, season, time of day, where attempt was made, time interval between attempt and discovery, and intent to kill. These factors are obviously related to the fact of an accomplished attempt, which explains the greater appropriateness of this scale for attempted suicide patients. It is noteworthy that the patient who rated highest risk by this scale, made an additional suicide attempt within thirty days of the study.

The Contra Costa "Suicidal Potential Evaluation" contains

Clinical Findings

five items of questionable value in terms of emphases in suicidology literature, and which provided little assistance in evaluating the young adult military suicidal patient. These five items are: "problem with alcohol," "drug addiction," "homosexuality," "the law," or "illegitimacy." The two final items, however, proved most helpful—"suffered a loss (death, separation, financial, self-esteem) within the last six months," and "come from a broken home."

On the whole, it would seem that one prediction scale may have been returning too low a risk score and the other possibility too high. For that reason, an alternative proposal will be offered in the applications section of chapter nine.

The "Goals of Life" Inventory provided further depth in perception of suicidal personalities. While the control group of this study, along with both the control and sample group of Carrigan's study, selected as their first choice, "D"—"Devotion to God, doing God's will"; the suicide patients selected "L"— "Giving love and security to one's family." This seems to say that suicide patients crave after that which has been hard to find in their lives, to the extent that meaningful human relationships take priority over the concept of relationship or obedience to God. The religious dimension of life, for the suicidal, thus appears to be the desire for a "hominized world," in the words of Johannes B. Metz. This is transition away from a more "cosmocentric" or "divinized world" to an "anthropocentric" world of man.[16]

The "Psychological Autopsies" show how often classical clues to suicide may appear in military young adult suicides. The basic dynamics at work in most of these cases were the same as described in most studies of male completed suicides. If one factor were to be singled out as possibly distinctive in these military cases, it would seem to be that in every instance a great struggle was experienced in efforts to prove oneself a mature, proficient, and acceptable man in a man's world. This struggle appeared to extend over many years, and possibly had its origin in relationship to the father figure at home. Military life may have simply brought this to a climax with its male and authority figure relationships.

NOTES

1. Navy Medical Neuropsychiatric Research Unit, "Percentages of Patient Groups with Suicidal Tendencies," San Diego, California, 1969. (Typewritten.)
2. Seiden, *Suicide Among Youth*, p. 33.
3. Durkheim, *Suicide* (1951), p. 237.
4. Long, *The World Almanac*, p. 167.
5. *Ibid.*, p. 169.
6. Tucker and Reinhardt, "Suicide Attempts," p. 17.
7. "Suicidal Potential Evaluation," Contra Costa Suicide Prevention Service, Walnut Creek, California, 12 December 1969. (Typewritten.)
8. Jacob Tuckman and William F. Youngman, "A Scale For Assessing Suicide Risk of Attempted Suicides," *Clinical Psychology*, XXIV, No. 1 (January, 1968), pp. 17-23.
9. *Ibid.*, p. 19.
10. Robert Lawrence Carrigan, "An Exploratory Clinical Study of the 'Religious Dimension' of Personality in Patients Hospitalized with the Disease of Ulcerative Colitis" (unpublished Th. D. thesis, Union Theological Seminary, New York, 1962), pp. 197-201. (Hereafter to be referred to as "Religious Dimension of Personality in Patients.")
11. Sidney Siegel, *Nonparametric Statistics for the Behavioral Sciences* (New York: McGraw-Hill Book Company, Inc., 1956), pp. 202-204.
12. Carrigan, "Religious Dimension of Personality in Patients," p. 203.
13. *Ibid.*, p. 209.
14. Siegel, *Nonparametric Statistics for the Behavioral Sciences*, p. 68.
15. Farberow and Schneidman, eds., *The Cry for Help*, p. 12.
16. Johannes B. Metz, *Theology of the World* (New York: Herder and Herder, 1969), pp. 57-60.

7. Treatment

ORGANIZATIONALLY

Research has indicated that when the "cry for help" is issued, it usually leads to successful suicide when answered by despair and dismay; but does not lead to suicide when hopefulness and help are the response. This was the lesson first learned by

Reverend Harry W. Warren one morning in 1906 in New York City. The night before, in a New York hotel, a woman urgently asked for a clergyman, but none could be located. When Reverend Warren, local Baptist minister, reached her the next morning in the hospital with serious injuries, she assured him she would not have injured herself if she could only have reached him the evening before. Reverend Warren fulfilled the last wishes of this dying woman when he founded the "National Save-a-Life League."[1] Today the organization is being run by his son and grandson, both of whom are likewise Baptist ministers.

At about the same time in 1906, the Salvation Army in England established an Anti-Suicide Department, which functions today as part of the Social Work Department of the Salvation Army.[2] This organization and the one founded by Reverend Warren are the two oldest Suicide Prevention Centers at work in the world today.

There were several other pioneering efforts in suicide prevention in Europe at the turn of the century, which are no longer in operation. From 1893 to 1906, the Lemberg Volunteer Rescue Society apparently operated in various cities of Germany, Austria, and Hungary.[3] During the 1920's the Welfare Department of the Vienna Police Department carried on considerable suicide prevention work.

The first medical scientific work on suicide prevention was begun in 1948 at the Vienna University Hospital for psychiatry under Dr. Erwin Ringel.[4] Soon afterward, in 1948, the Catholic Welfare Organization, working with Dr. Ringel, founded the *Lebensmüdenfürsorgestelle* (Suicide Prevention Agency). This emphasis was complemented by pastoral concern in London in 1953 when the Baptist pastor, Reverend West advertised, "Before you commit suicide, ring me up."[5]

Klaus Thomas tells how work begun in Berlin in 1953, under the title *Lebensmüdenbetreuung,* attempted to bring together medical, scientific, and pastoral concerns. A telephone service was also included. When all services were in full operation, Thomas says people were waiting in lines and counselors had to walk around the block to see them.[6]

It was also in 1953 that Chad Varah began his well-known work with the "Samaritans" in London. Personal and pastoral care by a "befriender" was the style of their service. Volunteers were trained and used in listening to and befriending one who threatened suicide. Success of the work soon spread to sixty-five branches through the United Kingdom and others around the world.[7]

In 1958, the Los Angeles Suicide Prevention Center was opened under the auspices of a five-year U.S. Public Health Service grant, with facilities in the Los Angeles County General Hospital.[8] It has served as the most extensively organized and widely functioning agency of its type in the United States. Under the leadership of Doctors Norman L. Farberow and Edwin S. Shneidman, the Los Angeles Center has conducted vital research, offered extensive services, and worked in close liaison with other community resources concerned about suicide.

Catholic Father Kenneth B. Murphey established "Rescue Incorporated" on March 1, 1959, in Boston City Hospital. A staff of seventy members includes psychiatrists, psychologists, physicians, ministers, rabbis, nurses, and social workers.[9] Like others, a twenty-four hour telephone service is crucial to the agency's work.

Alan Walker's Life Line Center in Sydney, Australia, established in the early 1960's, emphasizes the twenty-four hour telephone crisis service for suicide as well as other crises.

Since 1960, cities and hospitals alike have seen the great value and consistent results of a Suicide Prevention Service. Today there are reportedly over 130 Centers in operation across America. They range in size from the most modest with a budget at $10,000 per year (for one coordinator and small staff) to that of the Los Angeles Center with a budget of $300,000.[10] From small beginnings at the turn of the century in Vienna, New York, and London, has grown one of the most valuable of tools in the whole field of health services and crisis ministries.

The threat of suicide has long been a concern of the military services. For, unlike his civilian counterpart, whose actions may effect only a small number of people or fairly isolated social unit, the military man is part of many complex interrelationships and contributes to the efforts of a large group. For this reason, efforts have been made to provide the "captive" service community with adequate and readily available psychiatric services. Yet, as

Treatment

Dr. Hauschild indicates, the actual number of military suicides comes close to equalling civilian rates.[11]

Dr. Grissom of the United States Air Force stresses the efforts of military services to screen young men at the earliest portion of their basic training. It is at this point that he feels the problem is most acute. While other studies have indicated attempt rates, as compared to suicide, in basic training to be around 100 to 1, Dr. Grissom quotes 250 to 1 for the U.S. Air Force basic training population during the five-year period, 1964 to 1969.[12] Obviously, the vast majority of these people would be continued on active duty; and, according to one study, in rather successful fashion. Tucker and Gorman report that only 30 per cent of the suicidal patients returned to duty ever had critical comments registered by their supervisors.[13]

However, it is to be remembered that a high percentage of military suicidal patients manage, one way or another, to get out of military service before the end of their enlistment. This is generally accomplished only after these people have caused more trouble following psychiatric hospitalization. It would thus seem to behoove the welfare of the individual, the miltary service, and civilian communities where discharged men now return, if more effective management of the suicidal patient were possible in military service. The possibility of this will be discussed in section four of the eighth chapter.

Medically

From a medical standpoint, suicide tends to be viewed as a disease—a neurosis.[14] To deal with the neurosis a physician must watch for and indentify the predisposing factors. This is particularly important since research from the Fourth International Conference for Suicide Prevention in 1967 indicated that three-quarters of the patients, in a special study conducted in England, had seen a doctor within a month of their death and half of them had seen one within a week of their death.[15]

Apparently, it is very difficult for the physician to definitely identify signs of suicide. In this study just mentioned in England, 84 per cent of the suicides were reportedly suffering from depressive illness; yet antidepressant drugs were being prescribed for only one of the depressed patients.[16] Others were receiving barbiturates, tranquillizers, or no drugs at all. It looked as if the doctors failed to recognize the depression and were treating for anxiety or insomnia.

Another study by Litman with the therapists of 7,200 suicides noted an apparent repression in therapists which led to an impersonal reaction to the patient.[17] It was found that cases were often reviewed and presented to colleagues rather than dealt with in an active manner.

Dr. Sifneos says that when a doctor labels the suicide attempt as a "gesture," he usually discharges the patient without follow-up and rarely, if ever, asks for a psychiatric evaluation of the patient.[18]

A special concern is expressed by Dr. Havens when he says "that investigations of suicidal intent often stop short of taking up with the patient his attitude toward suicide."[19] Dr. Havens cites the research of the Los Angeles Suicide Prevention Center in saying that tactful discussion of suicide intent, far from proving harmful, can lead to detailed examination of the problem with new alternatives possibly emerging.

The first assistance to be rendered to the suicidal, says Dr. Robert Litman, chief psychiatrist of the Los Angeles Suicide Prevention Center, is counteracting the individual's feelings of hopelessness. He says:

> Psychological support is transmitted by a firm and hopeful attitude. We convey the impression that the problem which seems to the patient to be overwhelming, dominating his entire personality, and completely insidious, is common place and quite familiar to us and we have seen many people make a complete recovery. Hope is a commodity of which we have plenty and we dispense it freely.[20]

Dr. Morhauser points out that gaining time can be crucial in suicidal behavior, as in other forms of acting-out.[21] The patient may be told, he says, that there is always time to kill oneself. Simple postponement, for the present, may give time for vital insights and treatment.

Many suicidal patients will need the time, special care, and safeguards of hospitalization in which psychotherapy and electro-

Treatment

convulsive therapy may be offered.[22] Dr. Mathew Ross indicates how group participation activities may well be one of the mainstays in treatment.[23]

Special suicide risk should be recognized in depressed and schizophrenic persons with precautions provided, including assisting the family to understand possible dangers.[24]

Alerting families is considered important in all suicide cases, since the lethality rating is considered high for the first three months following any medical treatment.

In military medical practice, Tucker and Reinhardt recognize four forms of managing the suicide patient as follows:

1. Clarification of feelings and situations.
2. Reality confrontation.
3. Setting of limits.
4. Rapid return to duty with advice to patient's immediate superiors in regard to management.[25]

This approach, according to these two physicians, is similar to the form of management for general psychiatric patients. They further state that no rigid military policy determines patient management, but rather individual philosophy. Their own philosophy, they say, is directed toward aiding the suicidal patient to work on accomplishing tasks while limiting "the acting out."[26]

Laufer and Castriel emphasize that before the military medical officer can fully evaluate and treat a suicidal patient, witnesses, associates of the patient, and his superiors should be questioned. Questions should include:

> How long has the man been in the organization? What is his disciplinary and medical record? How often and how much does he drink? What is his general behavior—does he get into frequent fights; does he "blow his top" easily; does he mix with the other men or is he seclusive; what does he do in his spare time; and what are his habits? How is his mood—has it recently changed; has he appeared to be sad or depressed; does he do a lot of daydreaming or anything peculiar; has he received bad news lately; and has he appeared frustrated or asked for a transfer or shown any resentment about his duties? What is his intelligence level? What is his character and efficiency rating? Is he regarded as a good soldier?[27]

These doctors feel that if the above information is not obtained, the clue to proper diagnosis may be missed. When the diagnosis is made, the military physician, they say, is primarily responsible for the future of the patient only when the patient is (1) Psychotic, (2) Is overwhelmed by obsessive-compulsive neurosis, (3) Is neurotically depressed, or (4) Has a severe mental deficiency.[28] It is felt that patients who do not fit one of those categories must assume responsibility for their own behavior. Recommendation should be made say Laufer and Castriel to the administrative superiors regarding the amount of responsibility the patient must assume for himself. Commanding Officers are then left with final disposition.

It is both at this final point of disposition and at the very initial onset of crisis that the chaplain finds himself in a crucial position for rendering assistance.

Spiritually

Seward Hiltner says, "When a person asks, 'Why should I not take my own life?'; there is probably no ultimate answer except a religious one."[29] No doubt, among the 42 per cent of emotionally disturbed persons who seek a pastor to help them, many would be seeking that ultimate answer.[30]

Many are frustrated miserably in their efforts to find an answer of any meaningful significance about life. As one person said:

> There must be others like me who feel alienated, cut off from God, from a religion that seems to offer no help for their problems, their conflicts, their agonies . . .[31]

Someone else sought help and reported:

> I felt the need for spiritual help during a crisis. I traveled by bus to a church in Philadelphia hoping they would be having confessions at that time of day. They were, but unfortunately the priest stuttered and seemed nervous himself. Impatient people waiting opened the door to see if the box was empty. A fiasco.[32]

Treatment

Many fiascos ensue when the clergyman or layman of faith are called in life or death crisis and are found wanting. And they will be called upon. The Contra Costa Suicide Prevention Center, for instance, reports that of twelve resources they use in referring suicide callers, ministers and priests are number two, right behind psychiatrist, psychologist, or physician. The clinical findings of this present study indicate clergymen were asked for help by the suicidal more often than any other group. What resources, then, do men of faith have to offer those crying for help?

Chad Varah says of the suicidal, "They need love."[33] He says sometimes a client wants to be told of God's love, but these are few and far between; almost always "it is our love the client must be assured of."[34] This, says Varah, involves listening. He says if we can do nothing—we have borne it all with him and if "power has gone out" of us, the chances are it has gone into him.

Reverend Edward Stein says clergymen serve the suicidal in terms of preventive, supportive, and referral functions.[35] The first thing he would emphasize to clergymen is, "never minimize the fact that you are a constant symbol of hope in the world."[36] John Bonnell says, "The most powerful preventative of suicide is a firmly grounded religious faith."[37] To communicate hope and faith in a relationship of love, the clergyman must stay close to and know his people, says Stein. The clergyman needs to be available, watch for special stress situations, and involve persons in groups or meaningful activities to communicate acceptance.

Beyond these preventive measures, the pastor or person of faith, may bring invaluable supportive elements to the suicidal. The suicidal person needs concern, sympathy, and a firm positive and active response.[38] There must be a proper order in all this by which the pastor gives assurance of hope, listens fully to true deep feelings, and renders genuine support to the distressed. With this process, meaningful catharsis and acceptance may be experienced. Grollman would remind us that help of the clergyman on the suicide scene may bring "special authority" to the suicidal person, even possibly the authority of the father figure.[39]

Christensen says, "Talk about things worth living for, recall dreams unfulfilled, or persons who love and depend on him."[40] Through such sharing, a minister or priest can help the suicidal find proper perspective. It's possible that guilt may be banished, anger and depression be dealt with and overcome, forgiveness be accepted, and new beginnings be undertaken.

The clergyman should be especially alerted to expressions of high-risk potential. When a particular form of destruction is mentioned, for instance, the situation generally becomes acute. Persons giving such clues should not be left alone. In extreme cases of desperate confusion, the police or an ambulance service may be required.

The task of referral is an extremely important one for the clergyman. He needs to know the resources available, such as psychiatrists, psychologists, counseling clinics, suicide prevention services, or other special agencies for helping the distressed suicidal person. Referral to these resources, along with follow-up inquiry, and continuing supportive ministry to the patient, could prove life-saving. The crucial, after treatment time of risk, is when the ministry of one who is close and concerned could be decisive.

Like any other clergyman, the chaplain in military service has a wide range of opportunities to render preventative, supportive, and referral ministries to the suicidal. The chaplain may live a little closer to his people day by day, and thereby be able to more easily pick up important distress clues. There are periods for weeks and months when the chaplain, deployed aboard ship or living with men in the field, may be able to share with the suicidal or potential suicidal, in a meaningful depth relationship. The separation from families with accompanying loneliness poses unique challenges for the chaplain's ministry. Much of his concern and ministry to families will need to be sustained through correspondence. It may seem easy for the chaplain to get involved in "more than he can handle" in serious cases, yet in some isolated instances, the chaplain may be the only professional help immediately available.

Careful, patient, and compassionate listening may be the chaplain's greatest ministry to disturbed and suicidal persons. Openness, friendship, and warmth have long proven to be essentials of assistance to suicidal persons. These should be hallmarks in the ministry of relationships practiced by chaplains.

As with other clergymen, the chaplain offers a comforting

and healing ministry in the sharing of sacraments, services of worship, and private prayers. Many a man who is feeling alone and depressed, may find his spirits renewed in these spiritual ministrations.

The one who would bring spiritual ministrations to another in the depths of despair would want to remember and direct others to the source of spiritual life and power. Our God is the God of hope who has caused light to shine out of darkness, and can redeem life for anyone who calls upon His name.

The military environment does offer some opportunities of ministry and service to the suicidal patient, perhaps beyond most civilian communities. The organized, worldwide resources of the armed forces could be of vital assistance in treating suicide patients, as will be discussed in the next chapter.

INTERPERSONALLY

Civilian communities do, however, have the initial opportunity of providing counseling services and assisting persons in developing sound interpersonal relationships. There is, perhaps, no arena outside of the home itself so central to the individual and his problems as the public school or educational system. This section will deal, therefore, with the opportunities for counseling persons of suicidal tendency within the atmosphere of the academic setting. There is no reason, though, why these observations should not apply equally to counselors with young persons in church groups, youth centers, service clubs, or other community organizations. The premise at this point is simply that high school and college counselors will probably have more intense and longer exposure to persons in need than most other professional people in our society.

A brief survey of some pertinent findings will help focus the situation clearly before us. One of the first factors to impress itself upon the reader was clearly portrayed in a Denver study of adolescent patients hospitalized for suicide attempts. Almost three-fourths of the adolescents studies had an actual or threatened parent loss at the time of their admission to the hospital following a suicide attempt.[41] In addition, schoolwork was almost uniformly poor. Disciplinary problems were severe. Over two-thirds of the hospitalized adolescents had made one or two prior attempts at suicide. The loss of an object relationship—especially parent or boy or girl friend—appeared to predominate in precipitating causes.

Of special note in this Denver study is the evidence that the method of attempt was not significantly different between boys and girls. Ingestions were the popular method (28 of the 45 studied), with other methods equally used, proportionally, by boys and girls. A most striking finding revealed that forty-two per cent made additional attempts upon their life after hospitalization, with only slightly more attempts among the girls than among the boys.

An especially tragic picture may be seen among pregnant teenagers who, according to a Yale-New Haven Hospital study, may well be attempting suicide at a rate of roughly ten times greater proportion than other young female groups.[42] While society can be thankful that data suggests suicide carried to completion is uncommon during pregnancy, there is still grave danger of accidental completions especially when attempts reoccur. This danger is further accentuated because of the present attempt methods. The Yale-New Haven study indicates that ingestion is the method of attempt in fifty per cent of the occurrences. Other studies tend to confirm this percentage of ingestion of chemical agents in the under twenty age group. The wide usage of drugs in our society, especially unknown drugs and mixtures of drugs, has no doubt made availability of method a most pronounced factor.

According to Dr. Alex Barno, the most frequent psychiatric indication for therapeutic abortion is the fear of the patient committing suicide.[43] Again, thankfully, a sigh of relief may be in order as Dr. Barno's research asserts that most of these fears are unfounded. Data from his study show there were only fourteen suicides, one per 92,982 live births during a sixteen-year period. Ten of those suicides occurred post partum and only four occurred with the fetus in utero. None occured in illegitimately pregnant patients. Abortion may not thus be the first line of thought a counselor would want to pursue with the illegitimately pregnant teenager.

Shifting more specifically to observations on the college scene, we immediately encounter suicide in most disconcerting concentration. As cited in chapter three, among college students suicide is now the second greatest cause of death, with a rate fifty per cent higher than for other Americans of comparable age. They are the highest potential suicide risk group. In 1966, nearly 100,000 college students were reported to have threatened suicide; of these, one in ten actually attempted suicide, and 1,000 succeeded.

In a review of college suicides, Dr. Mathew Ross places considerable causal emphasis upon a deep sense of loss—loss of love, a parent, academic status, or a person of close relationship, thereby leading to a sense of isolation or alienation followed by anxiety, depression, and attempts at suicide.[44]

It may be helpful to realize the variation between male and female students regarding the college year in which suicide attempts seem to occur. A study of Harvard and Radcliffe students shows the men of Harvard having highest occurrence rates in the freshman year and lowest in the senior year, while Radcliffe's women had the lowest rates in the freshman year and highest in the senior and sophomore years.[45] The distribution is possibly explained by the men's frequent concern over problems with academic work, while the women most often reflected concerns with male-female separations. The latter is longer in developing and perhaps delayed in difficulty until later college years.

Researchers at the Harvard University Health Services have added an important note to drug usage by suicidal college students. While drugs have not been found to be the overwhelming problem behind suicidal behavior which many assumed, these findings from Harvard do specify that students chronically using a drug such as marihuana or LSD comprised fifteen per cent of the suicide attempt group in comparison to an estimated chronic usage rate of about four or five per cent in college population at large.[46]

In an article on college mental health services, Dr. Farnsworth states that more extensive mental health services probably lead to more accurate diagnosis and reporting of problems. This is perhaps most significant when the same report indicates that ninety per cent of the students who, in one study, attempted or threatened to kill themselves had been previously recognized as suicidal, and fifty-eight per cent of those actually committed suicide had been recognized as suicidal patients.[47]

During the First Annual Meeting of the Society for Adolescent Medicine, held in Washington, D.C., on 2 March 1969, Dr. Cizkova made an appeal for "advisory centers" to which young people could turn in time of psychologic crises.[48] He suggested these centers might be staffed by both professionals and volunteers with the mission of listening and talking with young people going through "The Suffering of Adolescence."

The University Center in Ann Arbor, Michigan, may well be an exemplary facility answering the needs by Dr. Cizkova. Beyond listening and talking, the University Center serves as a residential psychiatric treatment center for adolescents from seventh grade through college age.[49]

Such appeals and answers may pave the way to greater emphasis across the country for campus-supported facilities for group-centered approaches to suicidal and other emotional crises. This would obviously have the doubly beneficial effect of both bringing together trained resources and the strengths of social relationships, so often lacking among suicidal young people.

This approach to counseling and development of sound interpersonal relationships is also in tune with a key recommendation by Alvin Toffler in his work *Future Shock*. He appeals for what he calls "Coping Groups" across our society to help people undergoing the shock of change and readjustment in our mobile society.[50] If such adjustment groups are considered essential to the average contemporary citizen undergoing routine traumas of fast-paced society, surely the suicidal young person would need and benefit from them immensely.

Until the future comes, however, many counselors and workers with young people of high school or college age must look to resources at hand within themselves or within easy reach. What shall be their rod and staff in the face of the towering situation as portrayed?

In his book, *Group Leadership and Democratic Action*, Haiman has a section on leadership in interpersonal relations. In that section he speaks about "climate-making."[51] It just may well be that this is the central and all important task of individual, group, or institutional efforts to assist the young person in time of need. One needs to ask of the counseling scene, is the climate

Treatment

warm — open — concerned — patient — empathetic — responsive — understanding — and thereby truly therapeutic? The very arrangement of physical facilities is one thing mentioned by Haiman. An uninviting room, uncomfortable chairs, unpleasant surroundings, may "cool" a relationship from the very start.

And make no mistake—relationship is the alpha and omega of all efforts in counseling the suicidal individual. He or she would not be there except for a breakdown or total lack of meaningful relationship when it really counted. Many researchers have indicated or implied that the suicidal threat would never have been carried out had just *one* person been really close and expressed genuine concern. Dealing with the isolation that can lead to fatal depression, is the first task of any counselor or therapeutic group.

The amazing success of those who can achieve even a minimal relationship is testified to most eloquently by the country's Suicide Prevention Centers. In one twenty-minute phone conversation of concerned sharing, the Centers have achieved a record exceeding almost their own expectations in stopping suicides. Follow-up studies in several centers have confirmed the continuing positive results from thwarting momentary impulse and extending genuine concern and hope.

For when even a brief, passing relationship is established, the young person, as is true of any suicidal individual, is in some way asking, "is there any hope for my situation?" Failure to come through with clear, definite, and continuing assurance of a better resolution to one's problems might leave only one alternative to the despondent. That quality of hope which springs eternal is the preventative medicine for suicide.

But before even that medicine can be received, one may need to travel with an empathetic listener through the valley of every despair, heartache, and desperation known to man. The afflicted may wish to speak openly of suicidal intentions. These should never be taken lightly by the counselor, nor should they be cause for moving away from the subject. Ample evidence indicates the safety and fruitfulness of letting the distressed party talk out thoughts of suicidal intent.

At some calm moment of objectivity the counselor may wish to inquire further into the lethality or extent of suicide threat. This may be most accurately accomplished by use of a suicide prediction scale such as the ones referred to in chapter six or proposed for use with armed forces personnel. A discreet assessment of lethality will give the counselor clearer indications of whether private, group, or hospital therapy may be called for.

This implies, of course, the need to be willing and able to properly refer a disturbed person to adequate care resources. Several studies of mental health situations in America point to the fact that fewer referrals are made by counselors to other professional resources than would be expected. The suicidal patient or counselee may be a person most especially in need of wider, more intensive follow-up therapeutic relationships than any one counselor could ever hope to offer by himself.

A note may well be in order regarding an area of even more immediate and decisive consequence. There is a great tendency to see persons threatening suicide, or actually making suicide gestures or attempts, as simply manipulative individuals who are out to totally control the counselor and thereby gain purely self-centered goals.[52] As a matter of fact, that's exactly the case quite, quite often. And when it is, the counselor's human reaction is to become annoyed, impatient, and downright hostile toward such dominating maneuvers. To do so is to react to the suicidal person's illness rather than his true need. This situation may present as great a challenge to the counselor as any he faces, for it calls for response not natural to his own feelings and usually not compatible with sound counseling techniques. For once, the counselor needs to recognize manipulation and tolerate it—at least for a season. In the suicidal individual, manipulation is the absolute last resort. Every personal resource is threadbare. To turn the distressed person away at this point is only shortsighted weakness on the counselor's part and very possibly fatal in its effects. After initial support, acceptance, and communication of hope, a time may later come for facing manipulation and evolving other strengths; but at the outset, let the counselor realize this is the time to bear his cross for another's sake.

Those who counsel persons in an educational environment are perhaps most easily deceived by smokescreens. A word of caution is in order regarding the evidence concerning motivation in student suicides. Contrary to expectation, it is seldom academic problems or certainly academic problems by themselves which provoke suicidal acts. One needs to probe beyond any surface appearance of such difficulty till deeper relationships and personal crisis may be encountered and dealt with. Certainly at the college level, there is considerable evidence to indicate that inward crises very likely are rooted back in unresolved family disturbances or in broken peer relationships.

A meaningful, restored viable human relationship of mutual trust and respect is the chief deterrent to the desperation of suicide. Building such a relationship and helping one find such relationships with others is of paramount importance. To do so is to open doors to future hope and desires to build a good life.

When a sign of that process has begun, the concerned counselor will do well to keep the suicidal person in his thoughts, memories, and prayers. Care travels in many deep unobservable channels, and the day may come again when genuine caring concern will keep a faint heart from despair. It may also bring one back to dig again for life's resources. To share such processes will be the challenge and opportunity of one who hears and meaningfully responds to the "Cry for Help."

NOTES

1. Thomas, "Marriage Counseling, Suicide Prevention and Pastoral Care," p. 3.
2. Farberow and Shneidman, eds., *The Cry For Help*, p. 139.
3. *Ibid.*, p. 137.
4. Thomas, "Marriage Counseling, Suicide Prevention and Pastoral Care," p. 3.
5. *Ibid.*
6. *Ibid.*
7. Chad Varah, *The Samaritans* (London: Constable and Company Ltd., 1965), pp. 26-30.
8. Farberow and Shneidman, eds., *The Cry for Help*, p. 6.
9. *Ibid.*, p. 141.
10. Shneidman and Mandelkorn, *How to Prevent Suicide*, p. 25.
11. Hauschild, "Suicide in Europe," p. 252.
12. Grissom, Department of the Air Force letter, 15 December 1969.
13. Tucker and Gorman, "The Significance of the Suicide Gesture in the Military," p. 860.
14. Yolles, *The Tragedy of Suicide in the U.S.*, p. 4.
15. "Ways To Prevent Suicide," p. 418.
16. *Ibid.*
17. Hand and Meisel, "Dynamic Aspects of Suicide," p. 3010.

18. Sifneos, "Manipulative Suicide," p. 526.
19. Havens, "Diagnosis of Suicidal Intent," p. 420.
20. Shneidman, "Preventing Suicide," p. 4.
21. Morhauser, "Suicide," p. 10.
22. Ibid.
23. Ross, "Suicide Among College Students," p. 110.
24. Morhauser, "Suicide," p. 12.
25. Tucker and Reinhardt, "Suicide Attempts," p. 10.
26. Ibid.
27. L. G. Laufer and D. H. Castriel, "Suicidal Gestures in Occupation Personnel on Okinawa," *U.S. Army Medical Forces Medical Journal*, III (1952), p. 1825.
28. Ibid.
29. Seward Hiltner, "The Pastor and Suicide Prevention: An Editorial," *Pastoral Psychology*, XVI, No. 160 (January, 1966), p. 29.
30. "Memorial Counseling Center," p. 4.
31. H. H. Brunt Jr., "Organization of a Suicide Prevention Center," *The Journal of the Medical Society of New Jersey*, LXVI (February, 1969), p. 62.
32. Ibid.
33. Varah, ed., *The Samaritans*, p. 78.
34. Ibid., p. 68.
35. Edward V. Stein, "The Clergyman's Role with the Suicidal Person," *Journal of Pastoral Care*, XX (1966), p. 76.
36. Ibid.
37. John Sutherland Bonnell, "The Ultimate Escape," *Pastoral Psychology*, IX, No. 81 (February, 1958), p. 22.
38. Stein, "The Clergyman's Role with the Suicidal," p. 81.
39. Earl A. Grollman, "Pastoral Counseling of the Potential Suicidal Person," *Pastoral Psychology*, XVI, No. 160 (January, 1966), p. 47.
40. James L. Christensen, *The Pastor's Counseling Handbook* (Westwood, New Jersey: Fleming H. Revell Company, 1952), p. 75.
41. James T. Barter, Dwight O. Swaback, and Dorothy Todd, "Adolescent Suicide Attempts," *Archives of General Psychiatry*, XIX (November, 1968), p. 524.
42. Ira W. Gabrielson, Lorraine V. Klerman, John B. Currie, Natalie C. Tyler, and James F. Jekel, "Suicide Attempts in a Population Pregnant As Teen-Agers," *American Journal of Public Health*, LX (December, 1970), p. 2297.
43. Alex Barno, "Criminal abortion deaths, illegitimate pregnancy deaths, and suicides in pregnancy," *American Journal of Obstetrics and Gynocology*, XCVIII, p. 356.
44. Mathew Ross, "Suicide Among College Students," *American Journal of Psychiatry*," CCCVI, No. 2 (August, 1969), p. 223.
45. Graham B. Blaine Jr., Lida R. Carmen, "Causal Factors in Suicidal Attempts by Male and Female College Students," *American Journal of*

Psychiatry, CXXV, No. 6 (December, 1968), p. 835.
46. *Ibid.*
47. Dana L. Farnsworth, "College Mental Health and Social Change," *Annals of Internal Medicine,* LXXIII, No. 3 (September, 1970), p. 469.
48. Jirina Cizkova, "The Suffering of Adolescence," *Clinical Pediatrics,* VIII, No. 8 (August, 1969), p. 434.
49. Rita Burgett, Letter from The University Center, 1700 Broadway-North Campus, Box 621, Ann Arbor, Michigan, 48107, n.d. (Mimeographed.)
50. Alvin Toffler, *Future Shock* (New York: Bantam Books, 1971), p. 393.
51. Franklyn S. Haiman, *Group Leadership and Democratic Action* (New York: Houghton Mifflin Company, 1951), p. 132.
52. Edward L. Ansel and Richard K. McGee, "Attitudes Toward Suicide Attempters, *Bulletin of Suicidology,* No. 8 (Fall, 1971), p. 22.

8. Prevention

THEOLOGICAL CONCEPTS

John Bonnell tells of a young man who stood for eleven hours of agonizing suspense on an eighteen-inch ledge seventeen stories above the street on the front of the Gotham Hotel overlooking Fifty-fifth Street and Fifth Avenue in New York. The date was July 26, 1938. Among the young man's final words before jumping to his death were, "I wish someone could convince me that life is worth living."[1]

Deep down, **every** suicidal person is probably expressing that same wish. The meaning, value, purpose, and ultimate point to life is the question at issue in suicide. For this reason one could say that, in a certain sense, suicide begins as a theological problem. The person despairing of life is asking, "Is there any sense to existence?" "Is there any plan for my life, even in the midst of so great a misery?" "Is there really some ultimate One who ultimately cares about me?" After conducting a study of values among suicide patients, Elsa Whalley concludes: "The most significant value the suicidal patients seem to have lost is the concept of the unique, intrinsic worth and irreplaceability of every individual human life.[2] This, in its essence, is a theological crisis.

And by the same token, any ultimate solution or prevention of suicide needs to be a theological solution. Someone needs to convey to the distraught and bewildered that he is infinitely precious in the sight of God. This can apparently only be conveyed with meaning, if the suicidal believes he is precious in the sight of one who speaks for God. Value, fulfillment, acceptance, and creatively meaningful love relationships are the medicines of suicide prevention. These medicines find their origin in theology or the shared life of faith. It is no accident that clergymen have been instrumental in founding Suicide Prevention Centers. For the faith and hope in theology is the answer to doubt and despair in suicide.

How strange it is to hardly find such thoughts in suicide literature. While theology and faith have for centuries dealt with suicide, seldom has a theological stance other than "Thou shalt not . . ." been found in expression. To be sure, men such as Donne, Hume, and Voltaire raised questions and objections; but only as one comes to the bridge from the eighteenth century to modern thought is there a glimmer of positive, affirmative theological thought, as expressed in Immanuel Kant. One of the dominant ideas animating his philosophy was that human life is sacred and must be preserved. His concept of the inherent dignity of man as a person makes suicide inconsistent with reason. In his *Metaphysic* he writes: "To dispose of one's life for some fancied end, is to degrade the humanity subsisting in his own person, and entrusted to him to the end that he might uphold and preserve it."[3]

Contemporary theology, especially that which emphasizes the centrality and sacredness of persons, would say human life is created in the image of God and is to be lived in divine stewardship for His purposes. We are God's people, created by Him, and destined to relationship of love with Him and all his people. Jesus said, "I have come that you might have life and have it more abundantly."

Two streams of theological thought of somewhat different orientation, would appear important in bringing life to the suicidal. The first, based upon the findings of this study with military patients, is that this world of human relationships needs to be interpreted as the place of God's Kingdom. Love of neighbor, because God first loved us and created us as brothers, is crucial to seeing value in this life.

Secondly, the theological concepts of redemption and resurrection as often associated with eschatology are hopes and realities with which the suicidal needs to become acquainted. The literature from Jung to the present, reports impulses to suicide in order to achieve rebirth and rid oneself of the old. The heart of our Christian faith ought to speak to this need in giving assurance of renewal through Christ unto even everlasting life.

The concern for life and the sacredness of persons as created in God's image has prompted statements such as these from religious groups in America, as contained in the Los Angeles County Medical Association Handbook on Religious Attitude Toward Medical Practices:

> Baptist—"Suicide is generally considered a defiant act of deciding about one's death as though usurping divine prerogative."
>
> Catholic—"A person is bound to take all ordinary means of preserving his health and his life. He is not free to refuse what is regarded as the ordinary means to offset serious illness or injury which would be a danger to his life."
>
> Orthodox Judaism—"The right to die is actually the practice of Euthanasia which is regarded as outright murder."[4]

While something of the judgment stance customarily taken by religion and theological points of view can be seen in these statements, it is also apparent that basic and vital concern is directed to the preciousness of life. Along with these concerns is a reference to how free man is to decide or "usurp" the authority for terminating life. To deal with this is to raise questions of long standing which might best be handled, having set the theological framework, by moving on to a discussion of ethics.

ETHICAL CONSIDERATIONS

Whalley reminds us that an expressed suicidal communication states, "a decision is about to be made, but has not yet been made."[5] The direction of that final decision may depend very heavily upon what is decided about one's right to take his own life. The legal, theological, philosophical, and social responses to this issue have varied from one century to another and from place to place. Most recently in this country, the question has been raised in relation to euthanasia, as people have asked their physicians about the possibility of quick and easy death.

A simplistic or radical response to the question is a constant temptation, yet the issue is far too complex for such resolution. First of all, as McConnell suggests, the implicit inference from Durkheim to the present is that suicide is not simply an issue of personal ethics.[6] The example, pattern, and influence of a few can very well become imitated and virtually standardized throughout a culture.

Yet, is is important to have an open stance in perceiving varieties of meaning in the act of giving up one's earthly life. George Kelly, says McConnell, reminds us that the significant value in suicide depends on whether one is trying to terminate or validate life.[7] Socrates and Jesus are referred to as history's classic examples of life validation through ultimate self-sacrifice.[8]

James Hillman, likewise, speaks of "the soul's claims" and the priority of psychological life over physical life.[9] He feels there may be situations in which the physical life may have to be thwarted and left unfulfilled in order to meet the "pressing concerns with redemption."

From the earlier writings of Voltaire and Montaigne, French existentialism has campaigned for the freedom of the individual to make a decision for life or death.[10] Their assertion would be that suicide is man's ultimate freedom and his true mark of humanity, which must not be denied him.

In the last analysis, it must be said that man always retains the freedom to take his own life. Apparently, God chooses to allow it as a human possibility, and no man can force another to keep breathing. The freedom of choice is present. The only question is, "How should man use that freedom?" "Does he have the right to take his own life?"

In rare exceptions, it would seem, from the foregoing, that one might indeed validate and bring fullest meaning to his life and to others by giving up his life. Yet, life in itself is one of the most sacred and supreme gifts from God. We have been bought with a price; we are not our own. From the theological position of sacredness in personhood, the Judeo-Christian response is one of preserving life. One has the freedom, and in rare exceptions, the right to take his life; but that right would exist only as seen in accordance with God's will. The primary and pervasive right of man is to live—to live to the glory of God and in the service of his fellow man.

Hopefully, this ethical position, based upon Judeo-Christian convictions of sacredness for life and persons, would lead to positive concerns for life rather than negative judgments toward those despairing of life. Such a position would remove taboos and stigmas against victims and their families. It would eliminate social persecution and abolish legal prosecution. It would restore life to any who are mentally ill, rather than blaming them for resorting to the taking of life. Right or wrongness of an act would be determined more by the circumstances of individual cases, than by a set code of automatic answers. Concern for life and preservation of it, with compassion for the distraught in life, is the proposed ethical stance for a contempoary Judeo-Christian view of suicide.

EDUCATIONAL CONCERNS

If suicide and attempted suicide are to be reduced, along with the private and public tragedy they bring, increased educational efforts will have to be made. Such efforts will need to be guided in two directions. Attention will first be called for in areas of research, study, and case study work to advance the knowledge of workers in suicidology. Menninger gives the challenge in saying, "I believe our best defense against self-destructiveness lies in the courageous application of intelligence to human phenomenology."[11] The second educational area is the general public. Both information and appropriate attitudes need to be communicated to society if despair is to be averted and assistance rendered when needed.

Some exciting and productive advances appear to be taking place in education of workers in suicidology. Signs of progress abound—from establishment of the Johns Hopkins University course of study in suicidology, to creation in 1966 of a national Center for Studies of Suicide Prevention within the National Institute of Mental Health.[12] Research, indicative of the broad investigations underway, includes: group dynamics and suicide by Binns, Kerkman, and Schroeder;[13] vanillylc-mandelic acid in suicide urine by Gregora and Matous;[14] repertory grid study of the interpersonal significance of suicide by Ryle;[15] and suicide and the body image by Lester.[16] And yet, so much more is needed in a wide array of areas, if suicidal behavior is to be well understood, treated, and prevented.

Education of the public may prove more challenging and demanding than educational research. And actual prevention of suicide may depend a good deal more on public awareness than private research. Stengel expresses this by saying, "The degree of damage and outcome of a suicidal act may depend on outside intervention, irrespective of the seriousness of the suicidal intent."[17]

It was quite appropriate, therefore, to include a particular editorial in the October 1969 issue of *Christian Century*. It was titled, "Death Education Proposed For the Public Schools." The article related how the chaplain of Presbyterian Hospital in Charlotte, North Carolina, said, "Public school children need death education as much as they need sex education."[18] Surely the chaplain, David Wilkenson, would agree that a study of suicide and how to prevent it should be included in the study.

Other articles in magazines, professional journals, and newspapers can be found calling for education about death and suicide for all age groups. Dr. Dan Leviton, professor of Health Education at the University of Maryland teaches a unit on suicide in which he uses the movie, "The Cry for Help," along with discussion and other class materials.[19] This material and approach in study would be appropriate for almost any class or age level.

The armed forces are probably no further ahead than the general public in education on suicide; and, certainly, they are in no less need of it. Unlimited opportunity is available for such training both in Basic Training classes and throughout one's military career. Military personnel should be as well aware of clues to suicide and preventive measures as they are of artificial respiration, first aid, and defense against atomic, biological, and chemical elements. In brief simple fashion, every person can be taught that suicide is preventable. The verbal, physical, and personal action clues can be discussed. The instructor can emphasize how any evidence, clue, conversation, or threat of suicide should be taken seriously. Appropriate referrals to the physician, chaplain, or superior officer should be explained and encouraged as deemed necessary. Above all, every person can and should be made aware of how his response to others, quality of relationship, ability to hear out another's troubles, and genuine concern for another's welfare, could be of life-saving significance.

The entire public needs to be regularly informed of the services by the local Suicide Prevention Center near them. The immediate help, referral for counseling, and supportive services they offer should be familiar to all.

FACILITIES REQUIRED

Beyond a positive and creatively helpful theology, a balanced and meaningful ethic, and a widespread educational program, it is also essential to provide and sustain adequate facilities, which are skillfully manned, if effective suicide prevention is finally to be realized.

Society can already be grateful for the rapid expansion of Suicide Prevention Centers within the last two decades. Thousands of professionals and volunteers in this country and around the world are daily employed in life sustaining service to millions. This service has been extended from special phone centers to hospitals, campus health centers, shopping center ministries, and other special community help organizations.

Norman Farberow explains the vital role of these special facilities in saying, "Focused resources are needed for this focused crisis."[20]

In no segment of society could this statement carry more meaning than in the armed forces. For in carrying out their mission, the military services become a worldwide organization.

It is not always easy to mount focused resources for problems in scattered corners of the world. Even in centers of population, focused resources may be difficult to gather if the resources needed are scarce, in demand for other problems, or lack specialized training in the focused area of difficulty.

These factors lead to what is considered to be the chief proposal of this search, as based upon clinical research, working experience, and examination of relevant literature. In addition to medical and psychiatric services at hospitals, bases, and training centers throughout the armed forces, it is the recommendation of this thesis, based upon findings and their interpretation, that a worldwide Armed Forces Suicide Prevention Center should be established. Such a center, located perhaps at a central military medical facility or a joint interservice center, in liaison with the National Institute of Mental Health, would be the authoritative resource in dealing with suicide and attempted suicide by any member in any branch of the armed forces throughout the world. Autovon telephone services could place any command in immediate contact with the Suicide Prevention Center for purposes of expert consultation or referral to the nearest resource available in the command's area.

The value of such an Armed Forces Suicide Prevention Center would be monumental in terms of meeting immediate needs; but beyond that, there would also be almost unlimited possibilities for research, in-depth case studies, follow-up efforts, seminars, production of educational materials, and interdisciplinary sharing both within the armed forces and in the civilian community.

The ease with which such a service could be established in the armed forces makes the proposal all the more attractive. The personnel, building space, operational know-how, and budgetary requirements are already at hand in present military facilities. All that's required is a pooling of resources, focusing of effort, and publicizing of services throughout the military establishment.

With an easy-to-remember, well-publicized phone number, the Armed Forces Suicide Prevention Center, like those established in civilian prevention centers, would no doubt find itself much in demand. This demand would become ever more increased as its services, educational materials, and therapeutic results became known. With resources encompassing physician, psychiatrist, psychologist, social worker, chaplain, nurse, volunteer visitors, and staff of enlisted personnel—all on a seven-day-a-week, around-the-clock duty schedule, there is no reason why the United States Armed Forces should not produce the most effective and productive suicide prevention center anywhere in the world.

It is with a vision of that possibility and a hope for its fulfillment someday in the future, that we turn now to the conclusion, with its applications and indications for further study.

NOTES

1. Bonnell, "The Ultimate in Escape," p. 20.
2. Elsa A. Whalley, "Values and the Suicide Threat," *Journal of Religion and Health,* III (1964), p. 244.
3. Louis I. Dublin, *Suicide: A Sociological and Statistical Study* (New York: The Ronald Press Company, 1963), p. 127.
4. Committee on Medicine and Religion of the Los Angeles County Medical Association, *The Faith of Your Patients* (Los Angeles, California: Los Angeles County Medical Association, n.d.), pp. 1-2.
5. Whalley, "Values and the Suicide Threat," p. 242.
6. Theodore A. McConnell, "Suicide Ethics in Cross-disciplinary Perspective," *Journal of Religion and Health,* VII, No. 1 (January, 1968), p. 8.
7. *Ibid.,* p. 10.
8. Farberow and Shneidman, eds., *The Cry for Help,* p. 258.
9. James Hillman, *Suicide and the Soul* (New York: Harper and Row, Publishers, 1964), p. 23.
10. Louis I. Dublin, *To Be or Not to Be* (New York: Harrison Smith and Robert Haas, 1933), pp. 214-220.
11. Karl A. Menninger, *Man Against Himself,* p. viii.
12. Shneidman and Mandelkorn, *How to Prevent Suicide,* p. 10.
13. W. A. Binns, D. Kerkman and S. Schroeder, "Destructive Group Dynamics: Peculiar Interrelated Incidents of Suicide and Suicide Attempts," *Journal of the American College Health Association,* XIV (1966), pp. 250-256.
14. Z. Gregora and B. Matous, "3-Methoxy-4-Hydroxy-mandelic Acid in Suicide Urine," *Acta Universitatic Carolinae Medica,* XIV (1968), pp. 59-65.
15. A. Ryle, "A Repertory Grid Study of the Meaning and Consequences of a Suicidal Act," *British Journal of Psychiatry,* CXIII (December, 1967), pp. 1393-1403.
16. David Lester, "Attempted Suicide and Body Image," *Journal of Psychology,* LXVI (July, 1967), pp. 287-290.
17. Stengel, *Suicide and Attempted Suicide,* p. 71.

18. "Death Education Proposed For the Public Schools," Editorial, *The Christian Century* (October 29, 1969), p. 1372.

19. Dan Leviton, "The Need for Education on Death and Suicide," *The Journal of School Health*, XXXIX (April, 1969), p. 272.

20. Milo Benningfield, "A Review of Suicide Prevention Centers in the United States, *Pastoral Psychology*, XVI, No. 160 (January, 1966), p. 42.

9. Conclusion

APPLICATIONS OF THE FINDINGS

The applications of this study may be divided into two parts. The first portion is a statement of suicide theory which has emerged from this research. The second section consists of proposals for Christian ministry and suggestions for dealing with factors in military life which, according to this study, are most often involved in suicide occurrence among young adult military personnel.

Any theory of suicide must first of all take into account the complexity of factors involved in suicide or attempted suicide. In a cross section of people over a period of time, suicide occurrence is to be seen as both sociological and psychological in origin, with possible influences of religion, economics, biological disposition, and a myriad of unknowns added in. By its very nature, then, this problem should be viewed from the outset as one requiring the interdisciplinary resources of medicine, sociology, psychology, psychiatry, theology, and other helping professions experienced in dealing with human emotions and traumas.

Results of clinical findings in this research would indicate those resources need to be directed to a particularly focused point of difficulty among the complexities found in suicidal behavior. Other theories of suicide have increasingly approached this point; but, so far as available literature indicates, none have come to center upon it exactly. Durkheim focused on society

Conclusion

as the source of suicidal behavior; Freud felt the psychodynamics at work within the individual were crucial; Sullivan spoke of neither society nor individual responsibility for suicide, but looked to interpersonal relationships as being decisive; Menninger posited a "significant other" of a generalized nature.

From this point, one step further is recommended in the progression. It would appear from this study's findings that not interpersonal relationships, in general, are decisive; but that certain very specific ones are the primary impetus to suicide. Those key relationships, as revealed in this study, are the primary, intimate family relationships of father, mother, sister, brother, wife, or fiance. If one wants to find what prompted a particular individual in a particular society to turn, under pressure, to the pattern of suicidal behavior, then study must be directed to what was happening in the primary relationships. To be sure, other resolutions besides suicide might have been possible, but given the right setting, under sufficient stress, with means available, and the example of others, suicide becomes a strong option for finalizing the tragic consequences of devastating primary relationships. The traumatic relationship may not be at all obvious. As seemingly the case in many young adult males, the problems with father may extend to earliest years and be manifest in the present through a variety of impulses and expressions. Suicide, it might be said, then, is dealing not just with a "significant other," but with *the* "primary significant other."

As indicated in chapter seven, the Christian ministry may be most effectively expressed with suicidal persons in terms of preventative, supportive, and referral services. This implies an openness on the part of churches and clergymen to the needs of persons as expressed in their disappointments, hostilities, depressions, and anxieties. Persons comprising the circle of primary significant others are a focus of attention by the church as it ministers to families in their days of gladness as well as woe. The listening, understanding, and sustaining comfort of a compassionate ministry may well yield life-saving results.

Both civilian and military clergymen will find their ministries increasingly effective as they refer to and serve with other professionals in an interdisciplinary approach to dealing with suicide problems. Seldom will the clergyman find his singular efforts to be sufficient in long-range caring for the suicidal or potential suicidal. Community mental health services, hospital staffs, counselors in private practice, and suicide prevention centers are among the resources clergymen should be using in ministry to suicide patients.

Yet, it should be remembered, that resources are often limited. It is important to do something now in helping suicidal persons. A direct, immediate word of acceptance, understanding, and assurance of positive help, is of crucial importance. The suicide patient is not asking if any agency, distant professional, or even God cares, but, "Do you who are with me now really care about me?" It is important to continue caring until fully adequate assistance is assured.

The chaplain in military service has the privilege of going with those to whom he ministers into distant and dangerous places. His presence and word of support can be the sustaining difference when pressures mount. His listening in a confidential relationship may be one of the few outlets for aggression and hostility that otherwise might be turned inward. A word from the chaplain to the physician or psychiatrist often brings immediate attention to the "loner" who might be hesitant to speak of his problems.

Naturally, the chaplain must be trained and sensitive to the clues, symptoms, and treatment of suicide and potential suicide patients, as indicated in previous chapters of this study. The prediction scales used in chapter six, or a similar instrument, might be of assistance in determining the extent of care required. Often, the difficulty in primary relationships may indicate a need for total family counseling. The chaplain may render valuable assistance in counseling relatives of the suicide patient. The chaplain of sensitive understanding, who communciates an attitude of available willingness to help, will very likely find himself being called upon for ministry to both military member and his family.

When the cry for help comes to the chaplain, he will want to remember it is an appeal for life even while the verbalization may be about death. The chaplain has a message of hope, meaning, and sacred regard for persons, which should radiate a feeling of positive acceptance about life to one who has doubts.

Conclusion

When bitter shame, tragic failure, and seemingly unbearable agony have been poured out, the chaplain still stands for and has the opportunity to speak a word of hope. Inner resources may equip one to face what cannot be changed, which, without such resources, would be crushing. The chaplain also labors for the changes within one's environment which bring greater health, wholeness, and fullfillment to human life. Several environmental factors in military service might be profitably examined with possible benefit for suicidal persons.

The most obvious presenting factor of suicidal behavior in military service, as seen both in this and a number of other studies, is the variety of conflicts, problems, and incompatibility individuals have experienced in being in military service. Even these, in accordance with the theory of suicide suggested, can most often be traced to other initial problems in primary relationships. However, for these people, military service sets up situations of almost catalytic proportion in bringing about specific action. For this reason, support is hereby expressed for the already proposed effort of making the armed forces an entirely volunteer force. Even those who volunteer might be accepted first on a provisional contract for one year, with the full four-year enlistment granted only after both the member and the service deem such to be mutually desirable.

This next proposal is based upon the high incidence of poor job performance and low educational level demonstrated in this and other studies on the part of military suicide patients. It is herein recommended that considerably increased opportunity should be extended to personnel, from basic training on through all duty assignments, to partake of remedial learning experiences of both an academic and professional nature. While the military services already encourage participation in college credit correspondence courses and general military training courses, there is very little available to the man who doesn't enjoy learning because he doesn't learn easily and needs assistance for elementary beginnings. It's surprising how far a man can go in the military, sometimes, disguising very glaring weaknesses in this area. The men of highest military rank in this thesis study, as a matter of fact, needed the most help in understanding how to complete the "Goals of Life" Inventory.

Further applications of this study touch upon basic operations and support of the military services. Clinical findings of this research demonstrated clearly how upsetting continuous hardship tours of duty were upon both the men and their families. While the military services usually strive to retain a balance in "separated" and "accompanied" tours, circumstances, beyond combat, can often combine to produce a malfunction of this cycle. A proposal of this study is that maximum effort should be made to sustain equitable tours of duty for all personnel. The inherent stability and emotional well-being of such practice is readily apparent.

The supportive factor concerns military pay. This element repeatedly came to attention in the clinical findings with suicide patients. A number of military pay raises in recent years have made the financial situation for most military families at least manageable.

When this research was originally completed, the lower ranking, married military personnel in pay grades E-3 or below, were experiencing severe pay problems.[1] Thankfully, within just recent months, the situation has been repeatedly improved, to the point that virtually a whole new picture exists.[2] Formerly, a wife had to work, a man had to hold two jobs (even with a military schedule), debts piled up, and the standard of living was at best substandard. Families on state welfare often drew higher pay than military families. An enormous degree of stress has been removed from the man in service by government assurance that his family can attain a decent standard of living. Hopefully, this balance with civilian pay and prices will be sustained in the event of future inflation or rise in cost of living. If not, this financial factor could again become as dominant a matter of critical influence upon suicidal behavior as originally appeared in this study's research. Beyond the consideration of pay itself, there is continued need for assistance with financial management and planning before a problem develops to crisis proportions.

In the previous chapter emphases were suggested in regard to both general education of armed forces personnel on suicide prevention and establishment of a central Armed Forces Suicide Prevention Center. Expertly trained resources would

Conclusion

then be available for worldwide detection, treatment, and prevention of suicide among military personnel and their families. At the moment, it is exceedingly difficult to find anyone in military medicine, counseling, or therapeutic treatment who considers himself a thoroughly trained and experienced expert in Suicidology.

As one specific tool in an enhanced program of work with military suicidal patients of all ages, the following suicide potential rating is recommended. It is a combined result of clinical research, other available scales, and counseling experience (see Table 36, next page).

This scale is so designed as to be of assistance with either those who have attempted suicide before, or with disturbed personnel simply suspected of possible suicide tendencies. The scale can be administered and evaluated by physician, nurse, chaplain, or counselor of virtually any background working with military personnel. It is recommended, on a basis of comparison with other suicide potential scales, that a "yes" answer to between eight and ten questions be considered a high risk potential and any number above ten be considered a very high risk. Persons scoring twelve or more should not be left alone, and should be receiving therapeutic assistance.

IMPLICATIONS FOR FURTHER STUDY

The Suicide Potential Scale, just presented for armed forces personnel, has not been used with any patient group. An evaluation of its helpfulness as compared to other scales would be a contribution of further study.

Basic psychodynamics also await research among military personnel. The extent either aggression or dependency factors tend to account for suicidal behavior among the military population needs to be explored.

Undoubtedly, the avenues of that exploration would yield significant clues for understanding suicidal behavior in many sectors of society. Perhaps the father-child relationship has been too long overlooked in this connection. Some portions of this research have highlighted that question repeatedly.

This in turn points to others close at hand who in this study,

TABLE 36

Proposed Suicide Potential Rating
for Armed Forces Personnel

Is this person:
1. Forty-five years of age or older?
2. Male?
3. White?
4. Protestant?
5. Separated, divorced, or widowed?
6. In poor physical health?
7. In poor mental health?
8. Living alone?
9. In pay grade E-3 or below?

Has this person:
10. Been hospitalized in the last six months?
11. Suffered a loss within the last six months? (e.g., death, separation, financial, self-esteem).
12. Come from a broken home (death or separation from one or both parents before the age of sixteen)?
13. Been unable to complete high school?
14. Been separated from his immediate family over 50 per cent of the last three years?
15. Made a previous suicide attempt?
16. Made a suicide attempt during March, April, or May?
17. Made a suicide attempt with firearms or explosives?
18. Made a suicide attempt between 6:00 A.M. and 6:00 P.M.?
19. Spoken of making a suicide attempt now?
20. Mentioned a particular suicide method?
21. Written a suicide note at any time?

Conclusion

have been designated as "the" primary significant other. As in studies of alcoholism, where we've seen the crucial impact family members have on the alcoholic's reaction, so may we yet glean much deeper understanding of the suicide patient's family.

More follow-up studies with families, patients and prevention centers for several years following suicide attempts could prove valuable as indicators of meaningful treatment.

Is the widespread availability of drugs and their usage giving us new insights into the relationship between method and actual occurrence of suicide? This field may provide opportunities for definitive conclusions regarding such uncertain connections.

Is military suicide today really the altruistic type described by Durkheim? Research comparing findings of today with his theories might prove most enlightening.

While statistics have generally proven that suicide rates decrease in time of war, reasons for that decrease have remained rather speculative. Furthermore, little or no study has been conducted to date on suicide occurrence by troops actually engaged in combat. Fruitful results might await such specialized research.

And finally, statistical studies show extremely high suicide rates for armed forces personnel before World War I and between World War I and II. These rates were recorded as high as 60 or more per 100,000, with an especially high percentage of those suicides attributed to officer personnel.[3] No such high incidence was recorded in the civilian population for those years. For some reason, the military suicide and attempted suicide situation, as recorded since the Korean War, has shown marked decrease to the point of equalling or surpassing civilian rates in reduction. No explanation of why this is so has been found in the literature. Research revealing answers to this situation might be an invaluable contribution to suicide prevention both here and around the world.

Suicidology is a new and virtually limitless field for research, case study work, and exploration of relevant theories. In both military and civilian centers of study, the hour of significant findings is at hand. The explosion of knowledge in these last two decades should provide impetus to the dawning of a new age for prevention and treatment of suicidal behavior, not only among young adults, but for all people in all places.

NOTES

1. E-3, married and under 2 years of service, received $3,097.00 annually. E-3 over 2 years received $3,828.00. E-2 over 2 years received $3,384.00.

2. E-3, married and under 2 years service, now receives $5,529.60 annually. E-3 over 2 years now receives $5,763.60. E-2 over 2 years now receives $5,367.60.

3. H. L. P. Resnick, ed., *Suicidal Behaviors: Diagnosis and Management* (Boston: Little Brown and Company, 1968), p. 243.

Appendix A
Personal Interview Questions

(Complete Listing of Responses)

1. "Tell me a little bit about yourself."

Father, serviceman previously	1
Did not complete high school	1
Oldest child	1
Depressed	3
Makes friends easily	4
Likes sports	5
Likes church	1
Likes reading	2
Likes music	3
Confused	4
Nervous	1
Creative	2
Evil	1
Don't drink or smoke	1
No trouble in the military	1
Broken home	2
Did complete high school	2
Likes sport cars	2
Likes travel	2
Trouble in military	2

Personal Interview Questions

Likes mechanical	1
Likes school	1
Family trouble	3
Doesn't make friends easily	4
Doesn't like sports	1
Sexual problems	2
Tendency to moodiness	3

2. "Could you share with me something of your background?"

Broken home	7
Mentions father	12
Doesn't drink, smoke, or narcotics	1
Poor health	9
Trouble—military	1
Finished high school	5
Didn't finish high school	5
Oldest child	5
Youngest child	1
Good health	4
Likes music	1
Loner	1
Marriage trouble	1

3. "What was occurring in your life just before you came to the hospital?"

Military trouble	6
Cut wrist	6
Previous attempts	10
Attempt A.M. before noon	6
December	4
Depressed	6
Wanted to go home	1
Previous hospitalization	4
Drank poison	2
Girl friend, family trouble, or worry	11
Antagonistic toward military	2
Debts	4
Pills	12
Suicide notes	2
Attempt P.M. afternoon	2
Felt pressure	2
January	5
October	1
Attempt P.M. after 6:00 P.M.	8
Poor peer relations	1
Wanted to kill self	5
Fell from height	1
September	1
Razor blades (swallowed)	1

Appendix A

	February	4
	Nervous	2
4.	"What bearing has being in military service had on your situation?"	
	Service messed him up	4
	Can't stand it	3
	Scared (trouble)	3
	Don't understand	1
	Not doing good	2
	Service schedule ruined family	6
	More pressure	4
	Career	1
	Strain of separation	1
	Caused debts	3
	Immature associates	1
	Got in trouble	1
	Very little	1
5.	"Is there a particular person or group of persons you've found to be especially helpful to you in this time?"	
	Doctor	1
	Commanding officer	1
	No one	10
	Psychiatrist	1
	Neighbors	1
	Working supervisor	2
	Chaplain	2
	Minister	1
	Fellow patients	1
	Priest	1
	Lawyer	1
6.	"What are your plans and feelings about the future?"	
	Work	6
	Find girl	1
	Get married	1
	Try to be something	3
	Stay in one place	1
	Catch up on bills	4
	Have home	2
	Have kids	1
	Provide for family	3
	Discharge	4
	College or school	6
	Career	1
	Go home	1
	Travel	3
	No future	1
	Solve problems	1

Appendix B
"Goals of Life" Inventory Directions

The following is a list of sixteen "goals of life" that people have considered important. Some of these goals of life you will recognize as more important to you than are others. Other goals you may feel are more important to *other people* than they are to *you*. The purpose of this inventory is to number these statements, FIRST, in the order you feel most *other people* would consider them important, and SECOND, in the order *you* would rate them as important to you.

After first reading all of the statements on page 148, you will find it easier to make your selections by taking them in groups of four as suggested below. Use pencil so that you can erase and make changes if necessary.

DIRECTIONS FOR PAGE 148

(1) Choose the four statements that you think OTHER PEOPLE consider *most important* and number them in the boxes beside the statements (1, 2, 3, 4, where #1 is the *most* important).

(2) Choose the four statements that you think OTHER PEOPLE consider *least important* and number them in the boxes (13, 14, 15, 16, where #16 is the *least* important).

(3) From the remaining eight statements, choose the four you feel are *more* important to OTHER PEOPLE and number them in their boxes (5, 6, 7, 8).

(4) Number the last four statements in order of importance to OTHER PEOPLE, and place these numbers (9, 10, 11, 12) in the remaining boxes.

OTHER PEOPLE'S "GOALS OF LIFE"

Number the Life Goals below by following the Directions given on page 147.

Your Choices

☐ A. Self-sacrifice for the sake of a better world; giving oneself for others.

☐ B. Peace of mind, contentment, quietness of spirit.

☐ C. Serving the community of which one is a part.

☐ D. Devotion to God, doing God's will.

☐ E. Being genuinely concerned about other people.

☐ F. Finding one's place in life and accepting it.

☐ G. Achieving personal life after death; going to heaven.

☐ H. Discovering a way of personal communion with God.

☐ I. Making a place for oneself in the world; getting ahead.

☐ J. Doing one's duty.

☐ K. Being able to "take it"; brave and uncomplaining acceptance of what life brings.

☐ L. Giving love and security to one's family.

☐ M. Understanding oneself; having a mature outlook.

☐ N. Depending on a personal message from God.

☐ O. Disciplining oneself to a wholesome and clean way of life.

☐ P. Participating fully in the life and work of the church.

YOUR "GOALS OF LIFE"

Number the Life Goals as *you* would arrange them in importance BY FOLLOWING THE Directions given on page 147, substituting the word *YOU* wherever the words Other People appear.

Your Choices

- [ ] A. Self-sacrifice for the sake of a better world; giving oneself for others.
- [ ] B. Peace of mind, contentment, quietness of spirit.
- [ ] C. Serving the community of which one is a part.
- [ ] D. Devotion to God, doing God's will.
- [ ] E. Being genuinely concerned about other people.
- [ ] F. Finding one's place in life and accepting it.
- [ ] G. Achieving personal life after death; going to heaven.
- [ ] H. Discovering a way of personal communion with God.
- [ ] I. Making a place for oneself in the world; getting ahead.
- [ ] J. Doing one's duty.
- [ ] K. Being able to "take it"; brave and uncomplaining acceptance of what life brings.
- [ ] L. Giving love and security to one's family.
- [ ] M. Understanding oneself; having a mature outlook.
- [ ] N. Depending on a personal message from God.
- [ ] O. Disciplining oneself to a wholesome and clean way of life.
- [ ] P. Participating fully in the life and work of the church.

LIFE-GOALS RATING SCALE

Now that you have marked the life goals it would be helpful to know *your reactions* to each of them.

Read each of the sixteen goals again, this time placing the *letter* of each statement (A-P) somewhere on the scale below to show whether you Agree, Disagree, or have No Opinion about it. As you can see from the Sample Scale below, you may have several statements at the same place on the scale. Or you may neither completely Agree nor Disagree, yet have some opinion: for this reason, the smaller lines between have been provided.

Be sure to use the *letters* of the statements on the inventory to make your scale, and not the numbers you have written in the boxes. A sample rating might be as follows:

SAMPLE:

Completely Agree	D, H, M, O
....	G
....	G, L
....	
No Opinion (Neutral)	E, K, N
....	A, F
....	
....	C, I
Completely Disagree	J, P

THIS SCALE IS FOR YOUR USE:

Completely Agree ....

....

....

....

No Opinion (Neutral) ....

....

....

....

Completely Disagree ....

Bibliography

BOOKS

Andics, Margarette von. *Suicide and the Meaning of Life.* London: William Hodge and Company Limited, 1947.

Benedict, Ruth. *Patterns of Culture.* New York: Houghton Mifflin Company, 1934.

Bosselman, Beulah Chamberlain. *Self-Destruction.* Springfield, Illinois: Charles C. Thomas Publisher, 1958.

Capon, Robert Farrar. *Bed and Board.* New York: Simon and Schuster, 1965.

Christensen, James L. *The Pastor's Counseling Handbook.* Westwood, New Jersey: Fleming H. Revell Company, 1952.

Dalstrom, W. G. and Welsh, G. S. *An MMPI Handbook.* Minneapolis: The University of Minnesota Press, 1960.

Dublin, Louis I. *Factbook on Man From Birth to Death.* New York: The Macmillan Company, 1965.

_____. *Suicide: A Sociological and Statistical Study.* New York: The Ronald Press, 1963.

_____. *To Be or Not to Be.* New York: Harrison Smith and Robert Haas, 1933.

Durkheim, Emile. *Suicide.* Glencoe, Illinois: The Free Press, 1951.

Farber, Maurice L. *Theory of Suicide.* New York: Funk and Wagnalls, 1968.

Farberow, Norman L. *Bibliography on Suicide and Suicide Prevention: 1897-1957, 1958-1967.* Washington, D.C.: U.S. Government Printing Office, 1969.

_____ and Shneidman, Edwin S. *The Cry for Help.* New York: McGraw-Hill Book Company, 1965.

Fedden, Henry Romilly. *Suicide.* London: Peter Davies Limited, 1938.

Feifel, Herman, ed. *The Meaning of Death.* New York: McGraw-Hill Book Company, Inc., 1959.

Fenichel, Otto. *The Psychoanalytic Theory of Neurosis.* New York: W. W. Norton and Company, Inc., 1945.

Frankl, Victor E. *Man's Search For Meaning.* New York: Washington Square Press, Inc., 1963.

Gurin, Gerald; Veroff, Joseph; Feld, Sheila. *Americans View Their Mental Health.* New York: Basic Books, Inc., 1960.

Haiman, Franklyn S. *Group Leadership and Democratic Action.* New York: Houghton Mifflin Company, 1951.

Hendin, Herbert. *Suicide and Scandinavia.* New York: Grune and Stratton, Inc., 1964.

Hillman, James. *Suicide and the Soul.* New York: Harper and Row, Publishers, 1964.

Klausner, Samuel Z., ed. *Why Man Takes Chances.* Garden City, New York: Doubleday and Company, Inc., 1968.

Knight, James A. *A Psychiatrist Looks at Religion and Health.* New York: Abingdon Press, 1964.

Kobler, Arthur L. and Stotland, Ezra. *The End of Hope.* New York: The Macmillan Company, 1964.

Long, Luman H., ed. *The World Almanac.* New York: Newspaper Enterprise Assoc., Inc., 1971.

Maves, Paul B. *The Church and Mental Health.* New York: Charles Scribner's Sons, 1953.

Meerloo, Joost A. M. *Suicide and Mass Suicide.* New York: Grune and Stratton, Inc., 1962.

Menninger, Karl A. *Man Against Himself.* New York: Harcourt, Brace and Company, 1938.

Metz, Johannes B. *Theology of the World.* New York: Herder and Herder, 1969.

Resnik, H. L. P., ed. *Suicidal Behavior: Diagnosis and Management.* Boston: Little Brown and Company, 1968.

Rosen, George. *Madness in Society.* Chicago: University of Chicago Press, 1968.

St. John-Stevas, Norman. *The Right to Life.* New York: Holt, Rinehart and Winston, 1964.

Shneidman, Edwin S. and Farberow, Norman L., eds. *Clues to Suicide.* New York: McGraw-Hill Book Company, Inc., 1957.

_____. *Essays in Self-Destruction.* New York: Science House, Inc., 1967.

Siegel, Sidney. *Nonparametric Statistics for the Behavioral Sciences.* New York: McGraw-Hill Book Company, Inc., 1956.

Stengel, Erwin. *Suicide and Attempted Suicide.* Baltimore, Maryland: Penguin Books, 1964.

Tillich, Paul. *The Courage to Be.* New Haven: Yale University Press, 1952.

Toffler, Alvin. *Future Shock.* New York: Bantam Books, 1971.

Bibliography

Varah, Chad, ed. *The Samaritans*. London: Constable and Company Ltd., 1965.

Walker, Benjamin. *The Hindu World*. New York: Frederick A. Praeger, 1968.

JOURNAL, NEWSPAPER, MAGAZINE ARTICLES AND PAMPHLETS

Ansel, Edward L. and McGee, Richard K. "Attitudes Toward Suicide Attempters." *Bulletin of Suicidology*, No. 8 (Fall, 1971), pp. 22-28.

Barno, Alex. "Criminal Abortion Deaths, Illegitimate Pregnancy Deaths, and Suicides in Pregnancy." *American Journal of Obstetrics and Gynecology*, XCVIII (June, 1967), pp. 356-67.

Barter, James T.; Swaback, Dwight D.; and Todd, Dorothy. "Adolescent Suicide Attempts." *Archives of General Psychiatry*, XIX (November, 1968), pp. 523-527.

"The Better Way." *Good Housekeeping* (October, 1969), pp. 207-210.

Beall, Lynnette. "The Dynamic of Suicide: A Review of the Literature." *Bulletin of Suicidology* (March, 1969), pp. 2-16.

Benningfield, Milo F. "A Review of Suicide Prevention Centers in the United States." *Pastoral Psychology*, XVI, No. 160 (January, 1966), pp. 41-45.

Berblinger, K. W. "Suicide as a Message." *Psychosomatics*, V (1964), pp. 144-146.

Binns, W. A.; Kerkman, D.; and Schroeder, S. "Destructive Group Dynamics: An Account of Some Peculiar Interrelated Incidents of Suicide and Suicidal Attempts in a University Dormitory." *Journal of the American College Health Association*, XIV (April, 1966), pp. 250-256.

Blachly, P. H.; Disher, William; Roduner, Gregory. "Suicide by Physicians." *Bulletin of Suicidology* (December, 1968), p. 5.

Blaine, G., and Carmen, L. "Brief Communications: Causal Factors in Suicidal Attempts by Male and Female College Students." *American Journal of Psychiatry*, CXXV, No. 6 (December 6, 1968), pp. 146-149, 834-837.

Blau, Kim P.; Farberow, Norman L.; and Grayson, H. M. "The Semantic Differential as an Indicator of Suicidal Behavior and Tendencies." *Psychological Reports*, XXI, No. 2 (October, 1967), pp. 609-612.

Boisen, Anton T. "The Problem of Values in the Light of Psychopathology." *Journal of Clinical Pastoral Work*, II, No. 4 (Winter, 1949), p. 196.

Bollea, G. and Mayer, R. "Psychopathology of Suicide in the Formative Years." *Acta Paedopsychiat (Basel)*, XXXV (December, 1968), pp. 336-344.

Bonnell, George C. "The Pastor's Role in Counseling the Depressed." *Pastoral Psychology*, XXI, No. 200 (January, 1970), pp. 40-41.

Brunt, H. H. Jr. "Organization of a Suicide Prevention Center." *Journal of the Medical Society of New Jersey*, LXVI (February, 1969), pp. 62-65.

_____; Rotor M.; and Glenn T. "A Suicide Prevention Center in a Public Mental Hospital." *Mental Hygiene*, LII (April, 1968), pp. 254-262.

Bruyn, H. B. and Seiden, R. H. "Student Suicide: Fact or Fancy?" *Journal of the American College Health Association*, XIV, No. 2 (December, 1965), pp. 69-77.

Castelli, Jim. "Suicide—The Whispered Word." *The Catholic News* (New York), February 5, 1970.

Cerny, L. "Telephone Consultation for Children and Adolescents, Communication of Confidence." *Acta Paedopsychiat (Basel)*, XXXV (September, 1968), pp. 274-278.

Cizkova, J. "The Suffering of Adolescence." *Clinical Pediatrics*, VIII (August, 1969), pp. 433-437.

Colbach, Edward M. "Psychiatric Criteria for Compassionate Reassignment in the Army." *American Journal of Psychiatry*, CXXVII, No. 4 (October, 1970), pp. 508-510.

"Death Education Proposed For the Public Schools." *The Christian Century*. Editorial, October 29, 1969.

Eggertsen, P. F. "Suicide by Air Force Personnel 1958 to 1964." *Military Medicine*, CXXXIII (January, 1968), pp. 26-32.

_____. "Suicide, the Opaque Act." *Military Medicine*, CXXIII (January, 1967), pp. 9-17.

Eisenthal, S. "Suicide and Aggression." *Psychological Reports*, XXI (December, 1967), pp. 745-751.

Engelstad, J. Chr. Bull. "Suicides and Attempted Suicides in the Norwegian Armed Forces During Peace Time." *Military Medicine*, CXXXIII (June, 1968), pp. 437-448.

"Facts of Life and Death." U.S. Department of Health, Education, and Welfare No. 600 (1970), pp. 16-24.

Faigel, H. C. "Suicide Among Young Persons: A Review of its Incidence and Causes." *Clinical Pediatrics*, V (March, 1966), pp. 187-190.

Farberow, Norman L.; Shneidman, Edwin S.; and Litman, Robert E., "The Suicide Prevention Center." *Pastoral Psychology*, XVI, No. 169 (January, 1966), pp. 31-39.

Farnsworth, Dana L. "College Mental Health and Social Change." *Annals of Internal Medicine* LXXIII (1970), pp. 467-473.

Fisch, M. "The Suicidal Gesture: Study of 114 Military Patients Hospitalized Because of Abortive Suicide Attempts." *American Journal of Psychiatry*, CXI (July, 1954), pp. 33-36.

Freed, Herbert. "Occupational Hazards of Psyicians—Suicide." *Pennsylvania Medicine* (October, 1969), pp. 65-66.

Freud, S. "Mourning and Melancholia." *Collected Papers*, IV (1948), pp. 152-170.

Gabrielson, Ira W.; Klerman, Lorraine V.; Curries, John B.; Tyler, Natalie C.; and Jekel, James F. "Suicide Attempts in a Population Pregnant as Teen-Agers." *American Journal of Public Health*, LX, No. 12 (December, 1970), pp. 2289-2301.

Goldsmith, William and Cretekos, Constantine. "Unhappy Odysseys." *Archives of General Psychiatry*, XX (January, 1969), pp. 78-83.

Gregora, Z. and Matous, B. "3-Methoxy-4-Hydroxymandelic Acid in Suicide Urine." *Acta Universitatis Carolinae Medica*, XIV, No. 12 (1968), pp. 59-65.

Grollman, Earl A. "Pastoral Counseling of the Potential Suicidal Person." *Pastoral Psychology*, XVI, No. 160 (January, 1966), pp. 46-49.

Hand, M. H., and Meisel, A. M. "Dynamic Aspects of Suicide." *New York State Journal of Medicine*, LXVI (December 1, 1966), pp. 3009-3016.

Hauschild, T. B. "Suicide in Europe." *Medical Bulletin U.S. Army, Europe*, XXI (August, 1964), pp. 250-254.

_____. "Suicidal Population of a Military Psychiatric Center, A Review of Ten Years." *Military Medicine*, CXXXIII (June, 1968), pp. 425-436.

Havens, L. L. "Diagnosis of Suicidal Intent." *Annual Review of Medicine*, XX (1969), pp. 419-424.

Hendin, Herbert. "Black Suicide." *Archives of General Psychiatry*, XXL (October, 1969), pp. 407-422.

Hiltner, Seward. "The Pastor and Suicide Prevention: An Editorial." *Pastoral Psychology*, XVI, No. 160 (January, 1966), pp. 28-29.

Jacobs, J., and Teicher, J. D. "Broken Homes and Social Isolation in Attempted Suicides of Adolescents." *International Journal of Social Psychiatry*, XIII (Spring, 1967), pp. 139-149.

Johnson, Barclay D. "Durkheim's One Cause of Suicide." *American Sociological Review*, XXX, No. 6 (1965), pp. 875-886.

Kier, A., and Giffin, M. B. "Some Observations on Airmen Who Break Down During Basic Training." *American Journal of Psychiatry*, CXXII (August, 1965), pp. 184-188.

Kockelmans, Joseph J. "On Suicide: Reflections Upon Camus' View of the Problem." *Psychoanalytic Review*, LIV, No. 3 (Fall, 1967), pp. 31-48.

Langner, Herman P. "The Making of a Murderer." *American Journal of Psychiatry*, CXXVII, No. 7 (January, 1971), pp. 950-953.

Laufer, L. G., and Castriel, D. H. "Suicidal Gestures in Occupation Personnel on Okinawa." *U.S. Army Medical Forces Medical Journal*, III (1952), pp. 1825-1830.

Lester, D. "Attempted Suicide and Body Image." *Journal of Psychology*, LXVI (July, 1967), pp. 287-290.

_____. "Fear of Death of Suicidal Persons." *Psychological Reports*, XX (June, 1967), pp. 1077-1088.

_____. "Punishment Experiences and Suicidal Preoccupation." *Journal of Genetic Psychology*, CXIII (September, 1968), pp. 89-94.

_____. "Resentment and Dependency in the Suicidal Individual." *Journal of General Psychology*, LXXXI (July, 1969), pp. 137-145.

_____. "Seasonal Variation in Suicidal Deaths." *British Journal of Psychiatry*, CXVIII (1971), pp. 627-628.

_____. "Sibling Position and Suicidal Behavior." *Journal of Individual Psychology*, XXII (November, 1966), pp. 204-207.

Leviton, D. "The Need for Education on Death and Suicide." *Journal of School Health*, XXXIX (April, 1969), pp. 270-274.

Litman, R. E.; Curphey, T.; and Shneidman, E. "Investigations of Equivocal Suicides." *Journal of the American Medical Association*, CLXXXIV (1963), pp. 924-929.

McConaghy, N.; Linane, J.; and Buckle, R. C. "Parental Deprivation and Attempted Suicide." *Medical Journal of Australia*, I (May 21, 1966), pp. 886-892.

McConnell, Theodore A. "Suicide Ethics in Cross-disciplinary Perspective." *Journal of Religion and Health*, VII, No. 1 (January, 1968), pp. 7-25.

McCulloch, J. W., and Philip, A. E. "Social Variables in Attempted Suicide." *Acta Psychiatrica Scandinavica*, XLIII (1967), pp. 341-346.

_____; _____; and Carstairs, A. E. "The Ecology of Suicidal Behavior." *British Journal of Psychiatry*, CXIII (March, 1967), pp. 313-319.

Margolin, N. L. and Teicher, J. D. "Thirteen Adolescent Male Suicide Attempts." *Journal of the American Academy of Child Psychiatry*, VII (April, 1968), pp. 296-315.

Massey, J. T. "Suicide in the United States." *Vital Health Statistics*, XX (August, 1967), pp. 1-34.

Mitchell, A. R. "Suicidal Reaction in the Service Environment." *Journal of the Royal Army Medical Corps*, CIX (1963), pp. 215-219.

"Mortality Statistics; Suicides." *World Health Statistics Report*, XXI, No. 6 (1968), pp. 365-438.

"Most City Suicides Called Preventable." *New York Times* (September 26, 1971), p. 60.

Bibliography

Murphy, G. E.; Wetzel, R. D.; and Swallow, C. S. "Who Calls The Suicide Prevention Center: A Study of 55 Persons Calling on Their Own Behalf." *American Journal of Psychiatry*, CXXVI (September, 1969), pp. 314-324.

Neuringer, Charles. "Reactions to Interpersonal Crises in Suicidal Individuals." *Journal of General Psychology*, LXXI, No. 1 (July, 1964), pp. 47-55.

Newby, John H. Jr., and Van Der Heide, C. J. "A Review of 139 Suicidal Gestures: Discussion of Some Psychological Implications and Treatment Techniques." *Military Medicine*, CXXXIII (August, 1968), pp. 624-637.

Nossiter, Bernard D. "Suicide Ends GI's Cry: 'I Can't Stand All This . . .'" *The Washington Post*, September 25, 1969.

Oates, Wayne. "The Role of Religion in the Psychoses." *Journal of Pastoral Care*, III, No. 1 (Spring, 1949), pp. 29-30.

Offenkrantz, W.; Church, E.; and Elliott, R. "Psychiatric Management of Suicide Problems in Military Service." *American Journal of Psychiatry*, CXIV (1957), pp. 33-41.

Offer, D., and Barglow, P. "Adolescent and Young Adult Self-Mutilation Incidents in a General Psychiatric Hospital." *Archives of General Psychiatry*, III, No. 2 (1960), pp. 194-204.

Otto, U. "Suicidal Attempts Made During Compulsory Military Service." *Acta Psychiatrica Scandinavica*, XXXIX, No. 2 (1963), pp. 298-308.

Peck, Michael L. "Suicide Motivations In Adolescents." *Adolescence*, III, No. 9 (Spring, 1968), pp. 109-118.

Pokorny, Alex D. "Human Violence: A Comparison of Homicide, Aggravated Assault, Suicide, and Attempted Suicide." *Journal of Criminal Law, Criminology and Police Science*, LVI, No. 4 (1965), pp. 488-497.

_____. "Moon Phases and Mental Hospital Admissions." *Journal of Psychiatric Nursing and Mental Health Services* (November-December, 1968), pp. 325-327.

_____. "Moon Phases, Suicide, and Homicide." *American Journal of Psychiatry*, CXXI, No. 1 (July, 1964), pp. 66-67.

_____. "Suicide and Weather." *Archives of Environmental Health*, XIII (August, 1966), pp. 255-256.

_____. "Sunspots, Suicide, and Homicide." *Diseases of the Nervous System*, XXVII (May, 1966), pp. 347-348.

_____; Davis, Fred, and Harberson, Wayne. "Suicide, Suicide Attempts, and Weather." *American Journal of Psychiatry*, CXX, No. 4 (October, 1963), pp. 377-381.

Pozner, H. "Suicidal Incidents in Military Personnel." *British Journal of Medical Psychology*, XXVI, No. 2 (July, 1953), pp. 93-109.

"Prediction and Prevention of Suicide." *Canada Medical Association Journal*, C (May 10, 1969), pp. 867-868.

Pretzel, Paul W. "Suicide as a Failure of Trust." *Journal of Pastoral Care,* XXI (1967), pp. 94-99.

Primost, N. "Definition of Suicide." *Lancet,* I (February 11, 1967), p. 326.

Roche Laboratories. *Suicide Prevention: The Burden of Responsibility.* Nutley, New Jersey: Roche Laboratories, n.d.

Ross, M. "Suicide Among College Students." *American Journal of Psychiatry,* CXIII (August, 1969), pp. 220-225.

Ryle, A. "A Repertory Grid Study of the Meaning and Consequences of a Suicidal Act." *British Journal of Psychiatry,* CXIII (December, 1967), pp. 1393-1403.

Seiden, R. H. "Campus Tragedy: A Study of Student Suicide." *Journal of Abnormal Psychology,* LXXI (December, 1966), pp. 389-399.

⎯⎯⎯. *Suicide Among Youth.* Washington, D.C.: U.S. Government Printing Office, 1969.

Selzer, Melvin L., and Payne, Charles E. "Automobile Accidents, Suicide and Unconscious Motivation." *American Journal of Psychiatry,* CXIX, No. 3 (1962), pp. 237-240.

Shneidman, Edwin S. "Preventing Suicide." *American Journal of Nursing,* LXV, No. 5 (May, 1965), pp. 1-6.

⎯⎯⎯. "Suicide Among Adolescents." *California School Health* (October, 1966), pp. 1-4.

⎯⎯⎯. "Suicide, Sleep and Death." *Journal of Consulting Psychology,* XXVIII, No. 2 (1964), pp. 95-106.

⎯⎯⎯, and Mandelkorn, Philip. *How to Prevent Suicide.* New York: Public Affairs Pamphlets, 1968.

Sifneos, P. E. "Manipulative Suicide." *Psychiatric Quarterly,* XL (July, 1966), pp. 525-537.

Small, I. F., and De Armond, M. M. "The Clinical Assessment and Management of the Potential Suicide." *Journal of Indiana Medical Association,* LIX (November, 1966), pp. 1301-1306.

Spiegel, D.; Keith-Spiegel, P.; and Abrahams, J. "Humor and Suicide: Favorite Jokes of Suicidal Patients." *Journal of Consulting and Clinical Psychology,* XXXIII (August, 1969), pp. 504-505.

Stein, Edward V. "The Clergyman's Role With The Suicidal Person." *Journal of Pastoral Care,* XX (1966), pp. 76-83.

Strange, Robert E. and Arthur, Ransom J. "Hospital Ship Psychiatry in a War Zone." *American Journal of Psychiatry,* CXXIV, No. 3 (September, 1967), pp. 281-286.

⎯⎯⎯, and Brown, Dudley E. "Home From the War: A Study of Psychiatric Problems in Viet Nam Returnees." *American Journal of Psychiatry,* CXXVII, No. 4 (October, 1970), pp. 488-492.

"Suicide Among the American Indians." U.S. Department of Health, Education, and Welfare No. 1903 (June, 1969), pp. 1-37.

Tabachnick, Norman. "Interpersonal Relations in Suicidal Attempts." *Archives of General Psychiatry*, IV (1961), pp. 16-21.

Teicher, J. D. "A Study in Attempted Suicide." *Journal of Nervous and Mental Disorders*, CV (1947), pp. 283-298.

Tucker, G. J., and Gorman, E. R. "The Significance of the Suicide Gesture in the Military." *American Journal of Psychiatry*, CXXIII, No. 7 (January, 1967), pp. 854-861.

Tuckman, Jacob, and Youngman, W. F. "A Scale For Assessing Suicide Risk of Attempted Suicide." *Clinical Psychology*, XXIV (January, 1968), pp. 17-23.

United Press International. "Paris Girl, 17, Sets Self Ablaze, Leaps to Death." *The Sunday Star* (Washington, D.C.), January 25, 1970.

Varah, Chad. "Sexual and Religious Conflicts in Suicidal Young People." *Zeitschrift für Präventivmedizin*, X (1965), p. 10.

Vincent, Merville O. "Suicide and How to Prevent It." *Christianity Today*, X (1969), pp. 346-348.

Vital Statistics of the United States. U.S. Department of Health, Education, and Welfare, II (1967), pp. 80-86.

Wallis, G. G. "Attempted Suicide." *Journal of the Royal Navy Medical Service*, L (Autumn, 1964), pp. 155-158.

"Ways to Prevent Suicide." *Nature* (London), CCXX (November 20, 1968), pp. 417-418.

Whalley, Elsa A. "Values and the Suicide Threat." *Journal of Religion and Health*, III, No. 3 (1964), pp. 241-249.

Whitely, J. M. "Student Stress, Suicide and the Role of the University." *Journal of the Nation Association of Women Deans and Counselors*, XXX, No. 3 (1967), pp. 120-124.

Whitlock, F. A. "The Epidemiology of Drug Overdosage." *The Medical Journal of Australia* (June, 1970), pp. 1195-1199.

Yolles, Stanley F. *The Tragedy of Suicide in the U.S.* Washington, D.C.: U.S. Government Printing Office, 1969.

Zamcheck, N., and Geisler, M. A. "Homicides and Suicides of World War II." *Journal of Forensic Science*, V (1960), pp. 84-101.

UNPUBLISHED MATERIAL

Burgett, Rita. Letter from the University Center, Ann Arbor, Michigan, n.d. (Typewritten.)

Carrigan, Robert Lawrence. "An Exploratory Clinical Study of the 'Religious Dimension' of personality in patients hospitalized with the disease ulcerative colitis." Unpublished Th. D. dissertation, Union Theological Seminary of New York City, 1962.

Committee on Medicine and Religion, Los Angeles County Medical Association. "The Faith of Your Patients." A Handbook on Religious Attitudes Toward Medical Practices, n.d.

Contra Costa Suicide Prevention Center. "Report on Calls." Walnut Creek, California, June 21, 1965. (Mimeographed.)

Department of Pastoral Care. "Memorial Counseling Center." Information sheet of Memorial Hospital of Long Beach, California, n.d. (Mimeographed.)

Dietz, B. J. Letter from Chief, Bureau of Medicine and Surgery, Department of the Navy, Washington, D.C., November 23, 1971. (Typewritten.)

Grissom, Colonel Paul M. Letter from Office of United States Air Force Surgeon General, Washington, D.C., December 15, 1969. (Typewritten.)

Memorial Hospital of Long Beach. "Suicide." Information Bulletin of Pastoral Counseling Center, n.d.

Metropolitan Life. "Recent Trends in Suicide." Statistical Bulletin, New York, May, 1970.

Metropolitan Life. "Sharp Rise in Deaths Among Young Men." Statistical Bulletin, New York, August, 1969.

Mole, Robert L. "Vietnamese Buddhism." Unpublished Navy Personal Response Project Officer document of COMNAVSUPPACT, Saigon, FPO, San Francisco, California, 96214, n.d. (Mimeographed.)

Morhauser, E. G. "Suicide." Unpublished study for Medical Corps, United States Navy, Bureau of Medicine and Surgery, Washington, D.C., n.d. (Mimeographed.)

Munter, Preston K. "Depression and Suicide in College Students." Harvard University Health Service, Boston, Massachusetts, n.d. (Mimeographed.)

Navy Medical Neuropsychiatric Research Unit. Report on "Suicide and attempted suicide among young adults in the Armed Forces." Bureau of Medicine and Surgery, Washington, D.C., December 12, 1969. (Typewritten.)

Noel, Philip J. Jr. Letter from Office of the Surgeon General, Department of the Army, Washington, D.C., November 18, 1971. (Typewritten.)

Peck, Michael L., and Schrut, Albert. "Suicide Among College Students." Paper presented at the Fourth International Conference for Suicide Prevention at Los Angeles, October 19, 1967. (Mimeographed.)

Thomas, Klaus. "Marriage Counseling, Suicide Prevention and Pastoral Care." Unpublished lectures delivered at Wesley Theological Seminary, Washington, D.C., August 15, 1965. (Mimeographed.)

Tucker, Gary J., and Reinhardt, Roger F. "Suicide Attempts." Pensacola, Florida: Naval Aerospace Medical Institute, August 8, 1966.

Whalley, Elsa A. "Religion and Suicide." New York: Bureau of Research and Survey, National Council of Churches, February, 1964. (Mimeographed.)

Index

Abortion and suicide, 120
Aquinas, Thomas, 6
Adler, Alfred, 50
Adolescent suicide, 24, 47
Age factor, 20-24
Airplane suicides, 73
American Indian attitudes, 8-9
  Kwakiutl, 8
  Plains Indians, 9
  Pueblos, 9
American suicide problems, 53-54. *See also* United States occurrence
Armed forces
  aloneness, 57
  character and behavior disorders, 59
  dynamics, 57-59
  education, 58
  manipulative, 59
  occurrence, 38-42; vs. civilian occurrence, 40-41
  work, 58
Armed Forces Suicide Prevention Center, 134
Attempted suicide, 12
  suicide behavior or intent, 13
  suicidal gesture, 13
  suicidal ideation, 13
  suicidal threat, 13
Automobile suicides, 73

Barno, Alex, 120
Behavior patterns, 69-70
  mental health gauge, 70
  peculiar logic, 69
  withdrawal, 69
Biblical references, 6, 128
Bilanz-Selbstmord, 52

Broken homes as a factor, 55. *See also* Family life

Camus, Albert, 3
Chaplains
  ministry, 118-19, 138-39
  role, 138-39
Character and behavior disorders, 59-60
Christensen, James L., 117-18
Christian attitudes, 5-7, 26-27, 45
Church Councils, 6-7
Civil and Canon Laws, 7-8
College students
  academic factors, 56
  depression, 57
  drugs, 57
  dynamics, 56-57
  rates, 20, 38. *See also* Young adults, occurrence
  relationships, 57
College youth and suicide, 120-21
Commit compared to attempt, 41
Contemporary research, 132
Control group, 95
Counseling techniques, 122-25
Counteracting hopelessness, 114, 117, 119, 123, 139
Culture affecting method, 72

Daily patterns, 29-30
Death as life's goal, 4, 51
Definitions of suicide, 11-12
Depression in suicide, 54
Donne, John, 7, 45
Drugs, 74-77; and suicide, 121
Dublin, Louis I., 27, 51, 71
Durkheim, Emile, 11, 45, 48-50, 81, 130, 136

altruistic, 49
anomic, 49
egoistic, 48-49

Earliest theories of suicide, 45
Educational help, 139
Effects of marital status, 20
Eggertsen, P. F., 41, 60, 75
Equitable tours of duty, 140
Errors in reporting, 18
Evaluating and treating the suicidal patient, 115-16

Faigel, H. C., 55, 73
Family life, 107. *See also* Broken homes
Farberow, Norman L., 2, 22, 133
Farberow, Norman and Schneidman, Edwin, 2, 12, 24, 26, 51-52, 104, 112
Female methods of suicide, 76-77
Fenichel, Otto, 48
 guilt, 48
 superego, 48
Fourth International Conference for Suicidal Prevention, 113
Frankl, Victor E., 51
Freud, Anna, 47
Freud, Sigmund, 4, 45, 46-47, 52, 137

Goals of life inventory, 94-103
Greek and Roman suicide, 5
Grissom, Paul M., 113
Grollman, Carl A., 117

Hanging, 74-77. *See also* Violent methods of suicide
Hauschild, Thomas B., 38, 58-60, 66, 113
Hendin, Herbert, 25, 53
High and low risk category, 90-94
Hillman, James, 4, 51, 130
Hiltner, Seward, 116
Horney, Karen, 51

Immediacy of action, 138
India, 9
 Jouhar, 9
 Māmakham, 9
 Suttee, 9
Individual freedom, 7-8, 45, 130

Japan, 9
 harakiri, 9
Jung, Carl, 50

Kant, Immanuel, 128
Kelly, George, 51, 130

Laufer, L. G. and Castriel, D. H., 115-16
Lebensmüdenbetreung, 111
Lebensmüdenfürsorgestelle, 111
Lemberg Volunteer Rescue Society, 111
Lester, David, 55, 132
 sibling position, 55
Lethality of an attempt, 71
Life line, 112
Litman, Robert, 114
Los Angeles Suicide Prevention Center, 22, 52, 104, 112, 114
Male methods of suicide, 73-75
Managing the suicidal patient, 115
Meerloo, Joost, A. M., 3, 45
Menninger, Karl, 1, 12, 47, 131, 137
 three steps, 47
 significant others, 47
Mental health factor, 46, 52
Mentally ill rates, 20
Message of hope, 123, 138-39. *See also* Counteracting hopelessness
Metaphenomena, 53
Method and lethality, 71, 73
Middle Ages attitudes, 7
Military
 attitudes, 10
 life, 108
 pay, 140

Index

Morhauser, E. G., 5, 114
Murphey, Kenneth B., 112

National Save a Life League, 111
Newby, John H., and Van Der Heide, C. J., 59
Nonpsychoanalytic theories, 48-50

Occurrence
  by age, 34, 36
  by geographic area, 34, 37
  by sex and race, 34-35

Patient group, 79-87
  age, 81
  descriptive portrayal, 82-87
  marital status, 81
  race, 81
  rank, 81
  religion, 82
  work, 82
Peck, Michael L., 54, 56-57
Physicians' rates, 19
Places of occurrence, 31
Pokorny, Alex D., 29-31
Pregnant teen-agers, 120
Primary Significant Other, 137
Prodromal Clues, 66-68
  physical signs: body deterioration, 68; depression, 67-68; nervousness, 68; sleep, 68
  verbal clues, 66-67
Psychoanalytic theories, 46-48
  Eros, 46-47
  Thanatos, 46-47
Psychological autopsy, 104-7

Race factor, 25-26
Rado, Sandor, 48
  loss, 48
Rankings of suicides as cause of death, 18
Religion factor, 26-28
Religious attitudes toward suicide, 129. *See also* Suicide as sin

Rescue Incorporated, 112
Right
  to live, 131
  to take life, 45, 130-31
Ringel, Erwin, 111
Ross, Mathew, 5, 115, 121

Salvation Army work, 111
Samaritans, 111-12
Seasonal patterns, 28-29
Sex factor, 24
  commit vs. attempt, 24
Shneidman, Edwin S., 2, 3, 22, 52, 68. *See also* Farberow
Shooting, 74-77. *See also* Violent methods of suicide
Sifneos, Peter E., 54, 114
St. Augustine, 6
Stein, Edward, 117
Stengel, Erwin, 3, 51, 71, 132
Stoics, 5
Suicide
  notes, 52
  and primitive people, 3, 10. *See also* Taboos
  and the poor, 19
  as sin, 5-6. *See also* Religious attitudes toward suicide
  as theological crisis, 127-28
Suicide Potential Evaluation, 88-90
Suicide Potential Rating for Armed Forces Personnel, 141-42
Suicide Prevention Centers, 53, 123, 133
Suicidology, 2, 132, 141
Sullivan, Harry Stack, 50-51, 137

Taboos, 5-6, 11, 45, 131. *See also* Suicide, primitive people
Theological solutions, 128-29
Thomas, Klaus, 111
Tucker, G. J. and Gorman, E. R., 113
Tucker, Gary J. and Reinhardt, Roger F., 41, 59, 86, 115

Types of suicide
  chronic, 12
  concealed, 12
  focal, 12
  intentional, 12
  organic, 12
  semi-intentional, 12

United States occurrence, 1-2, 34, 37. *See also* American' suicide problems
Urban vs. rural rates, 19

Varah, Chad, 55-56, 111-12, 117
Vietnam, 9-10
  evidence, 60-62
  murder by oppression, 10
Violent methods of suicide, 71-72.

See also Hanging; Shooting
Volunteer armed forces, 139

Walker, Alan, 112
Warren, Harry M., 111
Weather effects, 30
West, Reverend, 111
Whalley, Elsa A., 7, 128, 130
World figures of suicide, 18
Worldwide occurrence, 32-34

Young adults
  dynamics, 54
  occurrence, 2, 36-39. *See also* College students, rates

Zamcheck, N. and Geisler, M. A., 39-40